Steven Ehrlich Houses

The Monacelli Press

Steven Ehrlich Houses

Text by Nancy Griffin / Introduction by Sam Lubell

Published in the United States by The Monacelli Press,
a division of Random House, Inc., New York

The Monacelli Press and the M design are registered
trademarks of Random House, Inc.

Library of Congress Control Number 2010942731
ISBN 978-158093-306-3

10 9 8 7 6 5 4 3 2 1

Printed in China

Designed by David Blankenship

Typeset in Proxima Nova

www.monacellipress.com

7 / Introduction by Sam Lubell

MASTERS

Kalfus Studio / 13

Addition to Neutra Beach House / 25

Schindler House on Ellis Avenue / 37

CITY

700 Palms Residence / 49

Webster Residence / 69

Boxenbaum Residence / 83

TREES

Schulman Residence / 97

Canyon Residence / 111

Waldfogel Residence / 125

VIEWS

Zeidler Residence / 143

Leonard Residence / 163

Carrillo Residence / 175

CULTURE

Wolfe Residence / 193

Helal Residence / 205

FUTURE: HOUSES IN PROGRESS

Kreuzer-Schroeder Residence / 223

McElroy Residence / 227

MacMillan Residence / 231

Project Credits / 236

Acknowledgments / 239

Illustration Credits / 240

For Steven Ehrlich, designing a house is always an adventure. He doesn't approach a project with any preconceived notions: he simply wants, as he puts it, "to find out what a house wants to be." Every home is a product of its site, its clients, and its surroundings, not of the whims of the architect or the style of the time.

Ehrlich, already passionate about the poetic forms of modern masters like Le Corbusier and Louis Kahn and excited about technical challenges from his education at Rensselaer Polytechnic Institute, learned this lesson early on, in what he says was the spark of inspiration for the rest of his work: the six years he spent in Africa, beginning in 1969. He began with a two-year stint in the Peace Corps in Morocco, explored virtually all of West Africa, and finally took a teaching position in Nigeria.

Here he was able to experience architecture that was formed not by ego, but by the constraints of its site and the inspiration of its culture. He was dazzled by settings like the luminous Zaria Mosque in Nigeria, the textured hill towns of Tunisia, the maze-like souks of Fez, the protected and intimate courtyard houses of Marrakesh, the gravity-defying raised forts of Ghana, and the interconnected desert cities of Algeria. All were formed through ingenious response to challenging contexts, and all had awe-inspiring qualities created by light, sound, and texture; a raw collection of attributes that created unforgettable experiences while integrating seamlessly into their environment and serving practical purposes above all else.

"It was a revelation for me. It was a whole new way of living, and it was so logical," says Ehrlich, who had grown up in the planned community of Radburn, New Jersey, far from the visceral impact and raw beauty of "Architecture Without Architects," as this type of construction was famously called by author Bernard Rudofsky. Elements like urban density, living without air conditioning, private gardens, rich materials, and the refinement of proportions all still influence Ehrlich's work. On his travels he also honed his love of adventure, and began cultivating tools from other architectural traditions. He would later carry on this cultural study in places like Asia and the Middle East.

When he returned to the United States in 1977, Ehrlich was uninvolved with the trendy forms of postmodernism; as he puts it, he was "from a more primal place." He was, of course, moved by his experiences in Africa, but he also held firm to his admiration for modernism, a movement that, with its focus on minimalism, honesty in materials, and an almost primal connection to the outdoors, echoed the indigenous architecture he had grown to love.

And once he had visited his sister in Los Angeles, he became fascinated with Southern California, in all its funky, experimental, ad hoc, outdoor-loving, pop-infused, and sometimes ugly glory, and it's still inspiring him today. "I love driving down Alameda Boulevard south of the 10 Freeway and looking at the funky car parts dealers that stack hub caps high into the sky. It's our culture." He adds, "I'm still intrigued by the layers of LA — the great neighborhoods, the fusions, the foods." The place encouraged architectural experiment for an open-minded clientele in a climate, landscape, and culture that nurtured it.

In the thirty subsequent years, little has changed about Ehrlich's approach to houses. Every project, combining the experiential and spatial lessons of vernacular architecture, the dynamism, purity, and innovation of modernism, and the immediate requirements of client and site, is still about "unlocking the potential" or "peeling away the onion." As he puts it, "How can we as alchemists of space and form and structure discover the inevitable?" And once that's been discovered, the other challenge is "falling in love with that idea" and making it something that is, above all, livable and likable to the client.

And that is the challenge with each house. There are commonalities in many of his residences — like spacious volumes, visual clarity, large windows, interlocking rooms, elements that continue from inside to outside, protected courtyards, structural honesty, richly textured materials, and a connection to nature — but each home is a new beginning, a chance to learn. A chance to soak up the place and its owners and create, more than anything, a spatial experience. Not an object, not a sculpture. But — like his inspirations in Africa — an experience.

"We never forget these are dwellings for people," said Takashi Yanai, who has worked with Ehrlich since 2002 and now heads his residential studio. "They're not purely formal exercises. We pride ourselves on the fact that they're architecturally challenging, and they are also good to live in." The spaces inspire, they lift the spirit, and they reflect the people who live in them more than the people who designed them. From additions to hillside houses to wooded sites to tight urban conditions, livability is always the focus.

Each house, as Ehrlich puts it, has its own "aha" moment, in which the pieces come together and the layers start to peel back. His first Los Angeles commission, the Kalfus studio in the Hollywood Hills, set out the process that Ehrlich continues to hone years later. The project, a guest house and art studio for Neutra's famed Loring residence, was designed to take advantage of its beautiful hillside site and provide large expanses of white space for hanging art. Instead of copying or competing with Neutra's horizontal and glassy residence, Ehrlich created a vertical counterpoint, a clean white box that takes advantage of glowing north light through huge window walls. The cube sites lightly on the landscape and provides an almost mystical sense of ethereality, like the original space. Ehrlich captured the north light but still maximized wall space by placing the glass walls to the north and east and installing a large sliding barn door to close the east window off if necessary. Like the courtyard homes of Marrakesh and the mosques of northern Africa, the project harnesses the feeling and even the weight of natural light and shadow to create intricate rhythms and a mesmerizing feeling. That light is perfect for the painting and photography that would be both produced here and hung on the walls.

The architect's first major ground-up residential commission was the Schulman Residence, a project for a well-known screenwriter and his family in LA's Brentwood neighborhood whose calm beauty is paired with its dramatic accentuation of site. Ehrlich was inspired by recent trips he had taken to Japan, from which he developed a formal palette that focuses on the environment and on natural materials — a snaking entry path, huge sycamore trees, ferns, an outdoor water spill, boulder-like rocks, copper overhangs, and mahogany window and door frames. But the real "aha" moment came after getting to know the site and realizing that the need to emphasize the axis to the wonderful canyon-front backyard. To do this, Ehrlich put the house at the narrowest part of the site and dug both the garage and one side of the house into the hillside. The house became a tool for exploring the wild landscape, protected by large trees and bursting with plants and animals. This scene is immediately visible inside through a double-story window wall with sliders that open up completely. The H-shaped house's two wings also have large sliding glass doors, so that the family can dine al fresco while still being inside. "You feel the presence of the outside in every room," explains Miriam Schulman. The family enjoys tracking the moon's shadows on the yard at night from the bridge over the large living room. "It's just glorious," she adds.

Twenty years later, Ehrlich is still experiencing these "voila" moments, as he also calls them. One of the firm's most recent residences is the Carrillo house in Pacific Palisades. After Ehrlich and Yanai got to know the family, they realized that, contrary to tradition, they should place the informal spaces in the front of the house and the formal ones in the back, taking advantage of the ocean views and creating separate zones for children and adults. They connected these areas via a tall room clad in stone with a floating wood roof and huge pivoting glass doors. Spaces meander informally into one another, an intimate sense of connection that is perfect for a family that likes to do everything together. "I love the flow of the house," says Juan Carrillo, who at first was concerned that the modern house might not be warm or of human scale but now is thrilled that it has both of these attributes. As with the Schulman house, all the rooms feel connected to the outdoors through large glass doors on the first floor and through wide window bands on the second. Still, like the courtyard houses of Morocco, the house maintains privacy in its tight urban site through tall bamboo stalks that rise high along the site's perimeter. The mix of stone, concrete, and glass makes the house feel both warm, proportional, and intricate while the careful balancing of light, which often peeks in through corners and skylights, creates a magical effect that evokes the light of an art gallery or chapel.

As such projects exemplify, Ehrlich's innovation often comes as a result of more subtlety than warping a facade or employing splashy colors. Often it comes about as a result of creating an unorthodox plan in which the house carves out open space, like the Webster residence in Venice, which creates a courtyard in a busy urban environment by breaking the house down into two masses or the Waldfogel residence in Palo Alto in which a pinwheel-shaped plan creates four distinct courtyards. The magic here comes not in formal gymnastics but in spatial choreography.

Another constant is material innovation, which, says Ehrlich, comes as a result of specific challenges, not for its own sake. "The technology is supporting some other goal. It's going to do a job." In Ehrlich's own house, in Venice, he created a 16-by-16 foot aperture that could accentuate the outdoors, making it feel like part of the living room, and allowing enough natural ventilation to exclude the need for air conditioning. "I wanted the glass to go away," describes Ehrlich, who worked with his contractor to create gigantic pivoting and sliding doors along the periphery of the large living spaces. "It took a lot of research," he notes. He had to ask questions like "What's the largest glass we can use? How minimal can we make the door thresholds? What's the budget?" He continues, "Architecture is so integrated to the fundamentals of materials and technology. It's about how do they work in concert with each other — not here's this idea, how do we make it work?"

Over the years the firm has been involved with many different types of projects, from office buildings to university structures. But still, says Ehrlich, houses, where the firm began, are its "backbone," providing the chance to experiment with ideas, details, and materials later used on much larger work. "We do our most refined detailing and finished concepts in our residential work," says Ehrlich. "That permeates into our institutional work." That approach often translates into large-scale work that includes warm materials like wood and stone, fine detailing, a close connection to the outdoors, and a more careful response to specific site than is often seen in institutional buildings. Elements like roll-up glass garage doors and zinc detailing, now common in the firm's non-residential portfolio, were both first used in residential work.

Ehrlich, Yanai, and their colleagues continue to peel back the possibilities of residential work, often inspired, not hindered, by the constraints created by clients and sites. For instance the upcoming McElroy residence in Laguna was hemmed in by an 11-foot height limit. So the firm decided to emphasize the horizontal, allowing all rooms to connect visually to the entry, and allowing rooms to open up with large glass sliders that make it feel as though the whole house is outdoors. Support spaces are buried underneath, allowing an uninterrupted feeling in the living areas.

This approach ultimately comes back around to the inspiration of Africa, where buildings are by their nature intimately connected to, and shaped by, their surroundings. Nothing is superficial; nothing happens without good reason. Buildings don't reflect a certain style, they are, like Ehrlich's work, timeless. All, Ehrlich says, comes down to the fundamentals of architecture. Refined proportions, materials, spatial relations. And powerful, poetic, experiences. It's what makes Ehrlich's architecture relevant no matter when it was made. And it's a bedrock on which his work firmly rests.

—

Julius Shulman
1981

Kalfus Studio

Los Angeles, California

A pristine cube set in the Hollywood Hills, the Kalfus studio was Ehrlich's first freestanding project in Los Angeles. The diminutive structure reflects both his passion for what he had seen and experienced in Africa and the powerful influence of California modernism. In Africa, Ehrlich had become enraptured with simple, primal forms and the way thick mud walls captured sunlight and cast shadows while taming the intense heat. Although he did not literally interpret this language of "architecture without architects," the Kalfus studio nevertheless conjures the spirit of Africa.

The clients, owners of Richard Neutra's Loring house, commissioned Ehrlich to design a separate painting/photography studio on the property that would also serve as a guesthouse. The site presented a precipitous canyon view and northern exposure. He was asked to make the most of the soft northern light, so conducive to making and viewing art, and provide generous expanses of white wall. A staff room and a sleeping loft were also part of the program.

At the time, the postmodern movement, with its anti-modernist zeal and affinity for color, ornamentation, and historical reference, was ascendant. But Ehrlich had not been privy to American architectural trends and had strong notions of his own. He wanted his building to engage in a friendly, rather than impertinent, dialogue with its modernist predecessor. He designed a spare two-story white box, establishing a vertical counterpoint to Neutra's one-story glass pavilion with its floating roof and strong horizontal lines. He chose materials and colors to complement the older house.

The white entrance wall is massive and unadorned, patterned by slatted shadows cast by a stair leading to the second floor. The modest doorway gives no clue to the drama within, a two-story volume drenched in light with a spectacular view of the wooded canyon. At the northeast corner fourteen-foot steel-framed paned windows converge and extrude from the cube, creating ever-changing patterned shadows throughout the day.

Julius Shulman
1961

Kalfus Studio

Kalfus Studio

Kalfus Studio

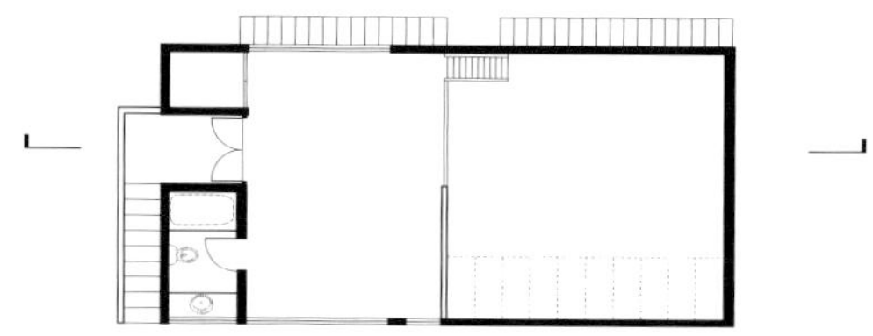

second floor plan

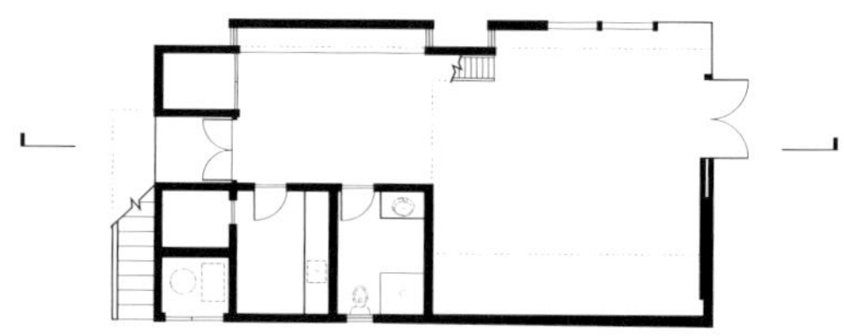

first floor plan

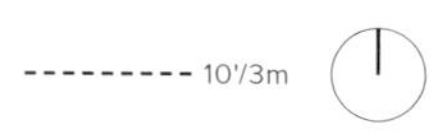

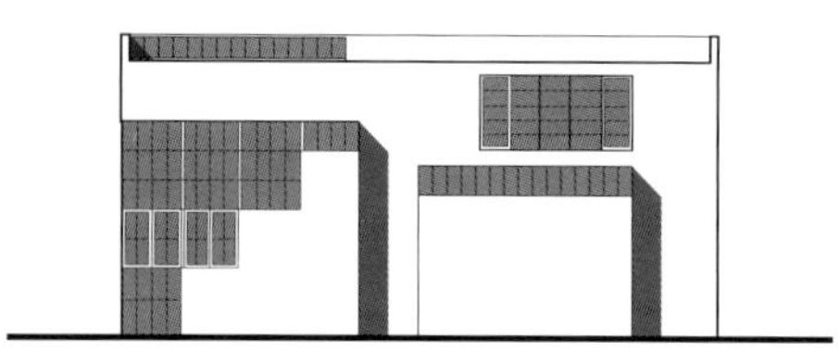

north elevation

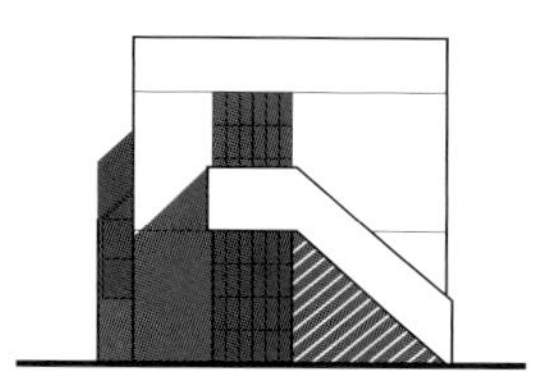

east elevation

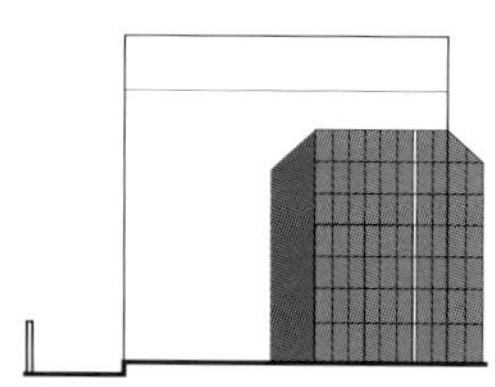

west elevation

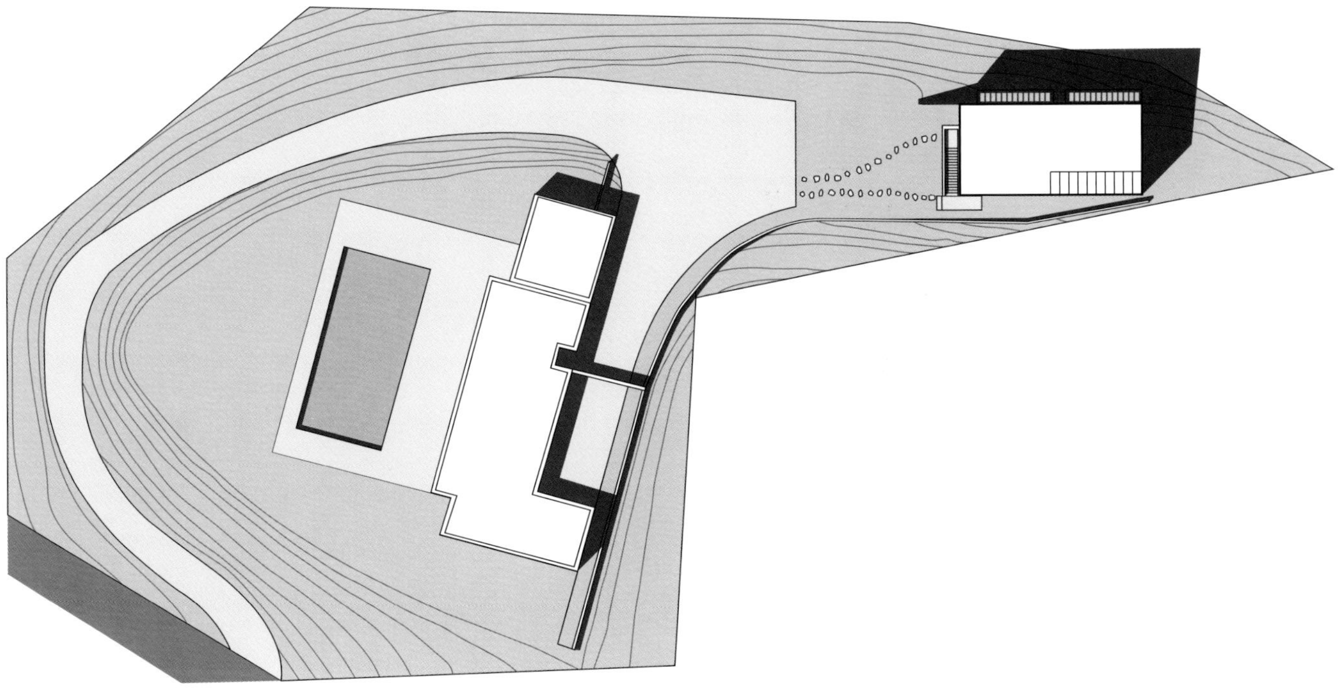

site plan

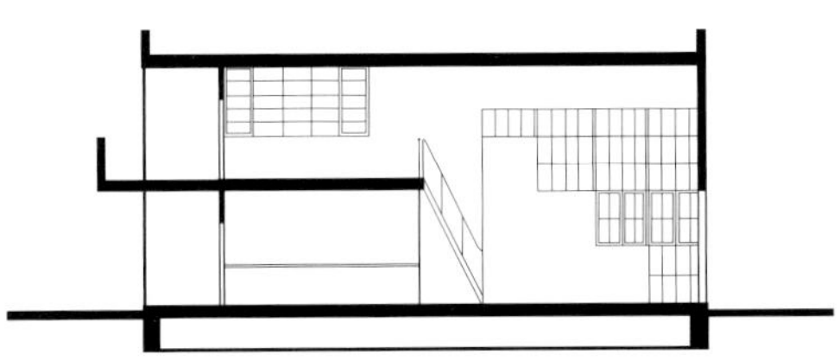

section

Kalfus Studio

Addition to Neutra Beach House

Addition to Neutra Beach House

Santa Monica, California

In 1938 Richard Neutra designed a beach house at the foot of a Santa Monica bluff, with breathtaking views of the Pacific Ocean. Originally built for an MGM movie executive, the Lewin house changed hands several times in succeeding decades and was once the home of Mae West, who shared it with her pet monkeys and decorated it with frescoes of male nudes.

The current owners, a couple with one child, purchased the adjacent lot and asked Ehrlich to design an addition consisting of a pool and entertaining area, with additional garage space, guest rooms, and staff quarters. The project also included restoration of the original house and relandscaping.

As a modernist, Neutra favored industrial materials including steel and concrete, but too often they were prohibitively expensive. This six-bedroom house was constructed of wood and stucco, which Neutra had painted in his favored palette of white and silver to make it look like steel. The wraparound windows of the semicircular front facade display the dynamic interpenetration of indoors and out that was Neutra's signature, offering panoramic views of the sea.

Sixty years later Ehrlich had access to high-tech materials and construction methods that Neutra could not even imagine. His intention was to design an addition that would honor the master's original work, while more fully realizing contemporary aspirations to lightness and transparency through the power of technology.

Ehrlich created a gossamer pavilion of steel and floor-to-ceiling glass, connected to the main house by a glass tunnel. At the end of each vault the glass can be retracted completely into a pocket between two concrete walls. Echoing the curve of the front facade, the space is capped by a soaring cycloidal arch that is an homage to Louis Kahn's Kimbell Art Museum in Fort Worth, Texas. Structural steel beams support the arch, making the dramatic volume possible, while a perforated stainless-steel ceiling modulates the acoustics.

The new garage with guest and staff rooms above is positioned in front of the house to form a barrier to the noisy Pacific Coast Highway. The pavilion nestles within the landscaped inner courtyard and lines up with the pool and perimeter wall on a strong visual axis. At the touch of a button, the stainless-steel wall on the far side of the pool retracts to frame a view of the beach and ocean.

Neutral colors throughout mirror the original house—but in the new building, they represent the natural hues of the cast-in-place concrete, stainless steel, and glass tiles, rather than painted surfaces. Details are restrained, including stretches of stainless-steel cupboards and a powder room sink that is a cycloidal arch in reverse.

Addition to Neutra Beach House

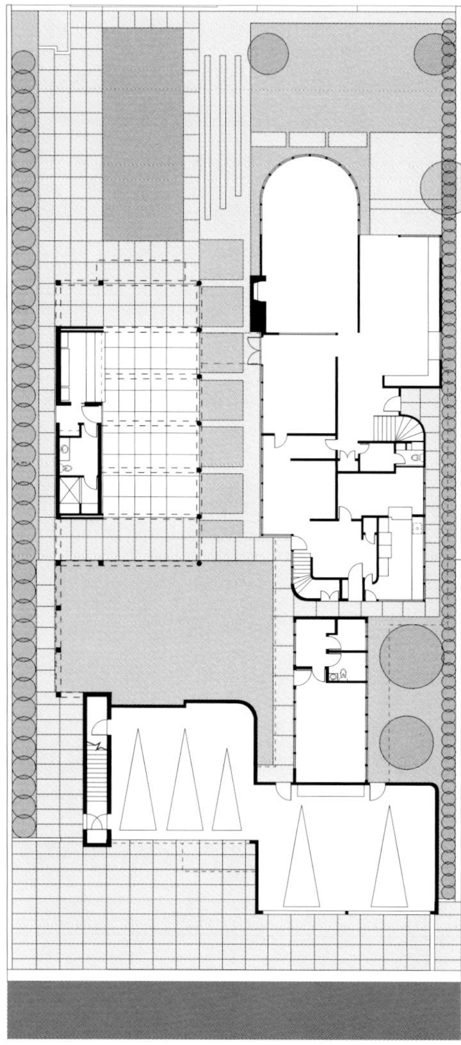

first floor plan

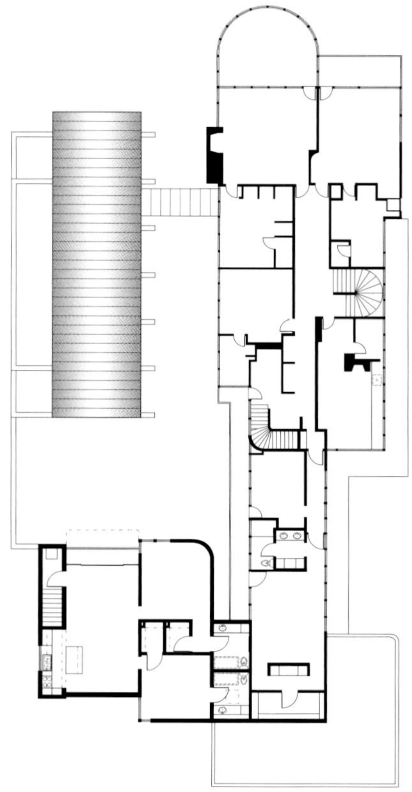

second floor plan

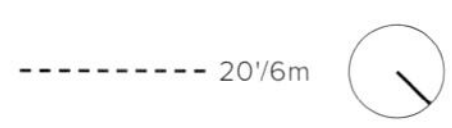

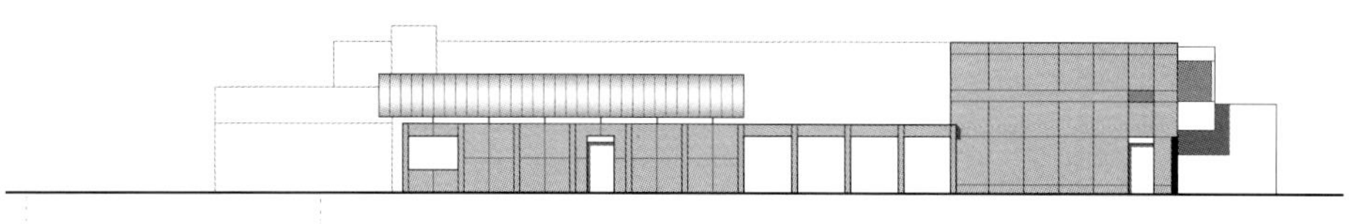

east elevation

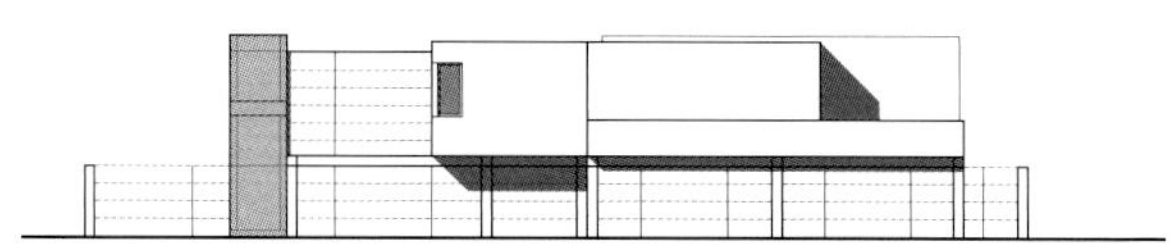

north elevation

site plan

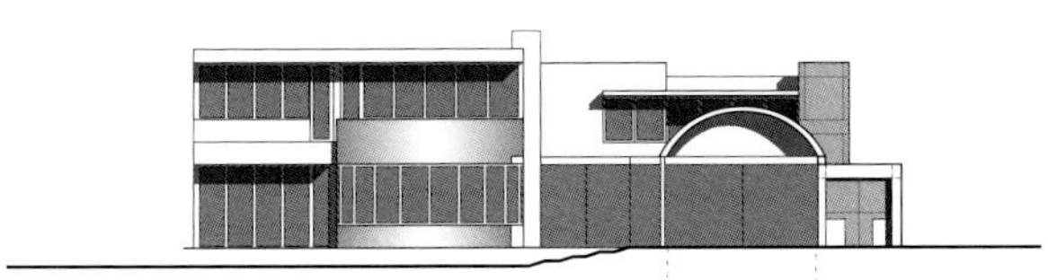

south elevation

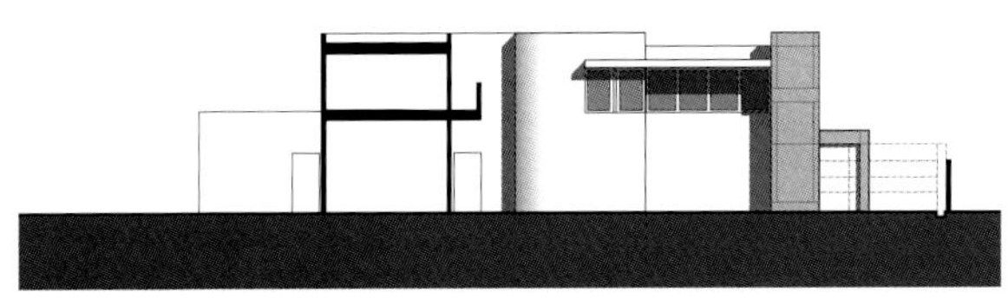

south courtyard elevation

Schindler House on Ellis Avenue

Schindler House on Ellis Avenue

Inglewood, California

This two-bedroom house, built in 1938, is one of three single-story stucco tract houses that Rudolf M. Schindler designed on a tree-lined street in Inglewood. The houses were similar but with slight variations adapted to the gently sloping topography.

When Ehrlich purchased the house, it was in such poor condition that saving it became a major rescue operation. Instead of a strict restoration that would freeze the design in time, he preserved the original design and details as much as possible while adding amenities so that a new family could live in and enjoy it. Confident that if Schindler were working today, he would take full advantage of current building technologies, Ehrlich made interventions that renewed Schindler's vision and updated it for a contemporary lifestyle.

Working with wood, plaster, and stucco and less than 1,000 square feet, Schindler had still managed to achieve a sublime spatial flow. Steps lead down from the entrance into an open living room with fireplace, a built-in desk, and floor-to-ceiling sliding glass doors leading into the generous rear garden. Clerestory windows in the bedrooms draw in abundant light while maintaining privacy.

In the renovation, plywood built-in closets and furniture were refinished and the brick-and-plaster fireplace was meticulously restored. A brick patio was relocated to the back of the property to create an outdoor living and dining area. Inspired by the sleeping porches of Schindler's iconic 1922 Kings Road house, Ehrlich fashioned a galvanized steel trellis above the patio and trained a seventy-year-old grape vine on the property to grow around it and provide shade.

To restore the crisp lines of Schindler's exterior stucco walls, which had been marred by crumbling plaster-and-metal rain caps, invisible waterproofing membranes were installed. Asbestos ducts were torn out and new insulation, heating, and air-conditioning introduced. Wooden door and window frames survived intact and were fitted with new tempered glass. The tiny kitchen, inadequate by today's standards, was opened up to the living room and fitted with new cabinetry and appliances. The original bathroom, judged to be without historical significance, received a total facelift as well.

There was evidence that Schindler had intended that the house share a front garden with its adjacent near-twin. The new owners collaborated on fresh landscaping, planting a drought-resistant succulent garden that presents a sustainable and neighborly alternative to suburban lawns.

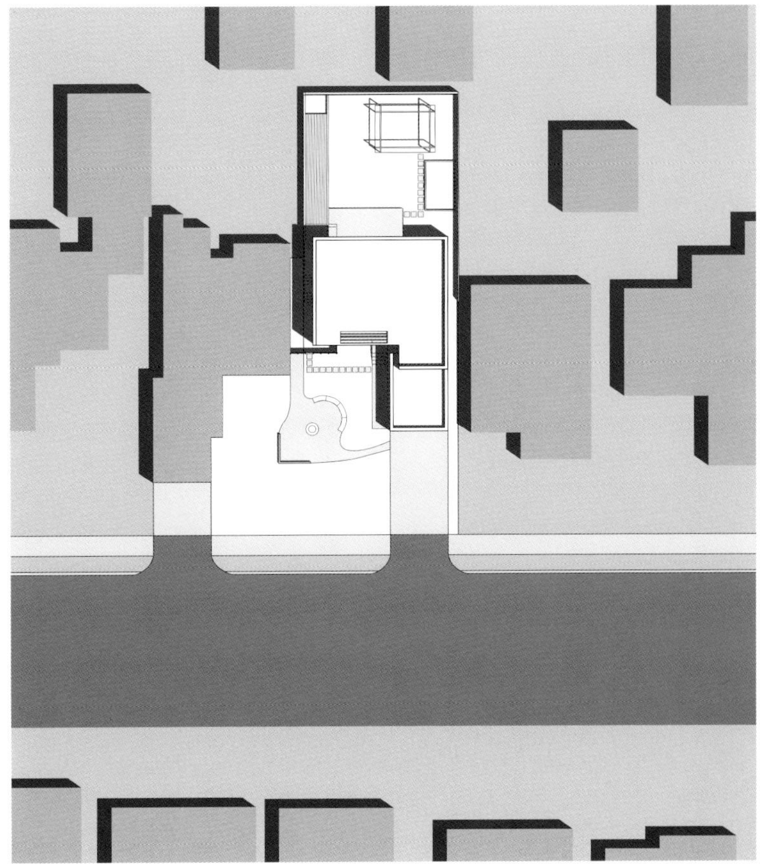

site plan

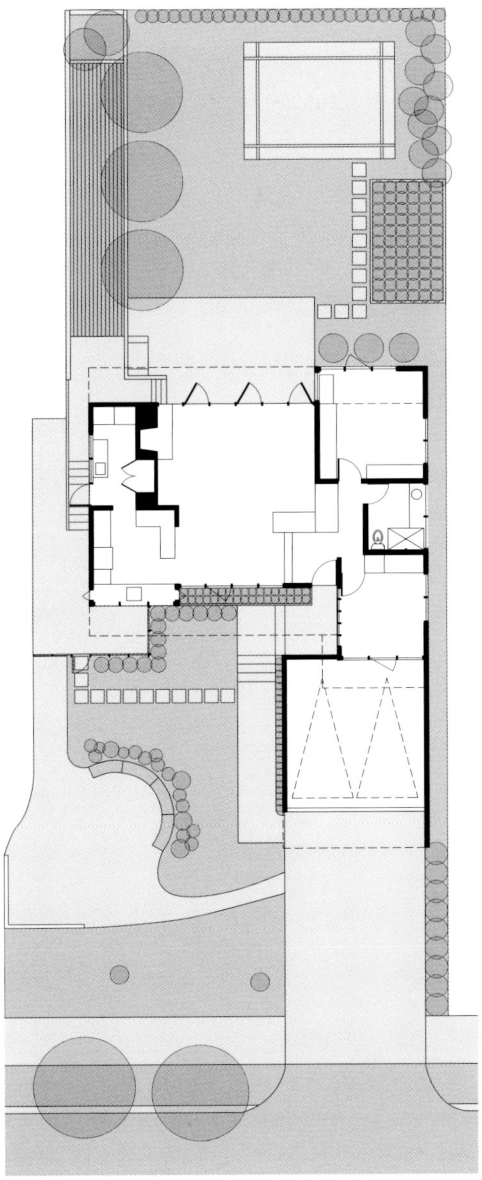

first floor plan

WOLF

700 Palms Residence

700 Palms Residence

Venice, California

When it came to building a house for himself, Ehrlich combined all the ideas he had been exploring in his residential practice in one exuberant statement. The 700 Palms residence integrates the primal earthiness of his African experience into a twenty-first-century expression of sun-drenched California modernism, utilizing the latest steel and glass technologies.

He purchased a lot in the lively, eclectic community of Venice, one of the few walking communities in greater Los Angeles, lured by its many shops and restaurants and its proximity to the Pacific Ocean. Ehrlich desired a private and environmentally sustainable compound for himself and his wife, with a separate guesthouse, which would entice his three grown daughters to visit frequently. The house needed to be cozy for two people but flexible enough to accommodate extended family visits and entertaining for large groups.

The design responds to the narrow (132 by 44 feet) site and three mature existing trees—two Aleppo pines and a Canary Island palm—which Ehrlich was determined to save. He established privacy within the dense urban fabric with an exterior perimeter fence, made friendly by the use of a translucent plastic material. Then he defined three internal courtyards around the location of the trees. The small front garden showcases the larger pine, which becomes a living sculpture; a lap pool is squeezed into the entrance courtyard on the side of the house; and the back garden features a raised concrete seating area and barbecue. At the rear of the lot is a two-story guesthouse and studio.

Space is calibrated within the house for maximum efficiency and dramatic impact. The low-ceilinged entrance explodes into the sixteen-foot-high main living-dining room. A glass bridge hung from narrow steel cables spans the volume, connecting two small second-story "pod" bedrooms with floating stairs to the master suite and study on the third floor.

The house is strikingly transformative, with large expanses of glass that open on three sides, with a combination of pivoting, sliding, and disappearing pocket doors. On sultry days the house becomes a breezy pavilion. A steel exoskeleton is fitted with electrically operated canvas shades that open and close to temper the sun and turn the pool court into a sheltering tent; their warm hues recall the colors of yarn hanging to dry in the souks of Marrakesh.

NO
PARKING
9AM TO 11AM
THURSDAY

700

The lightness and transparency of the main interior volume is anchored by a monolithic wall of white cement and pumice that constitutes the fourth side of the house. Low-maintenance, honest materials are used throughout and allowed to weather naturally. Exterior walls of Cor-Ten steel have acquired a rusted patina, siding is of recycled Trex (made from sawdust and plastic), and interior plaster surfaces are waxed and left unpainted. The poured concrete floors are pigmented with rich brown iron oxide. Built-ins include a tonsu stair and kitchen cabinetry of warm walnut.

The house relies on natural ventilation, capturing the breezes and remaining cool even during summer heat waves. Radiant floors indoors and in the outdoor concrete platform heat efficiently and roof photovoltaics harness the energy of California's abundant sunshine. Water-efficient irrigation systems and drought-resistant plantings are installed in the courtyards.

700 Palms Residence

Palms

700 Palms Residence

700 Palms Residence

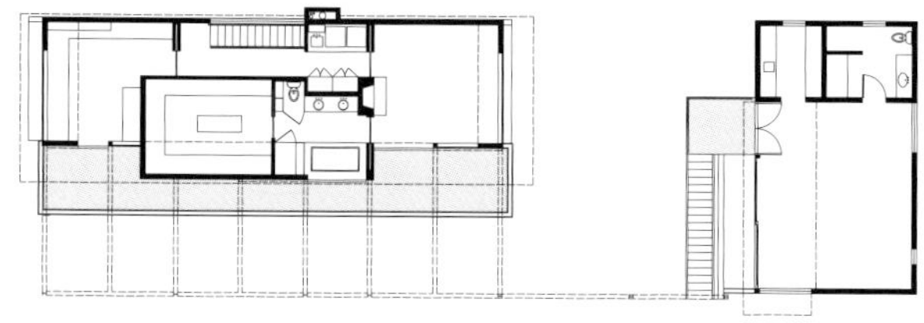

second floor plan

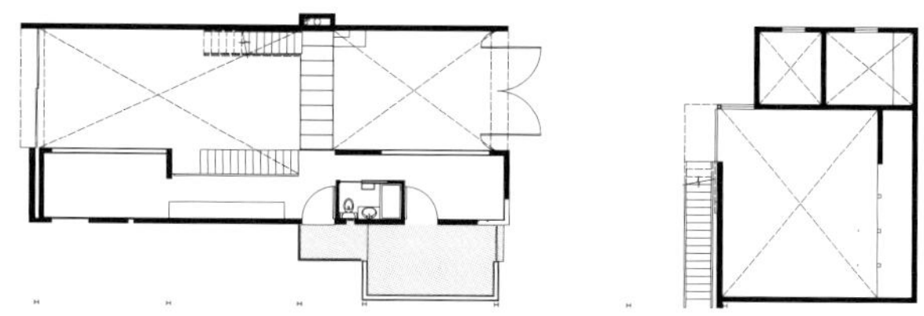

mezzanine plan

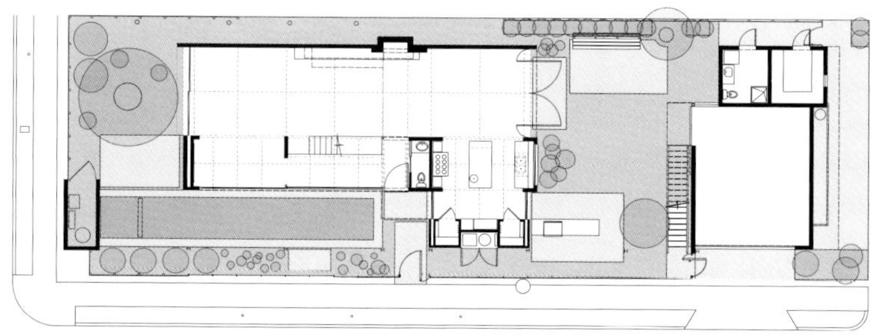

first floor plan

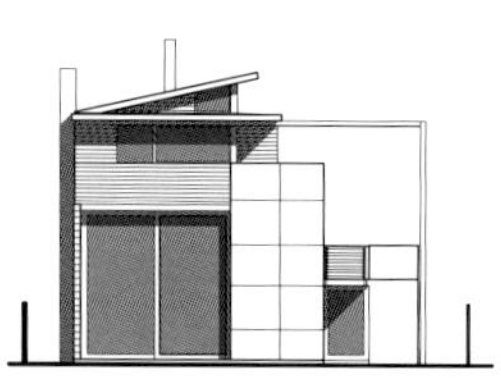

west elevation

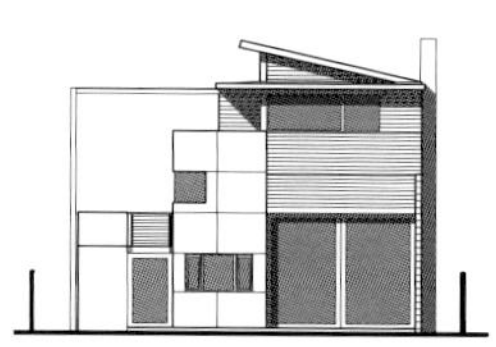

east elevation

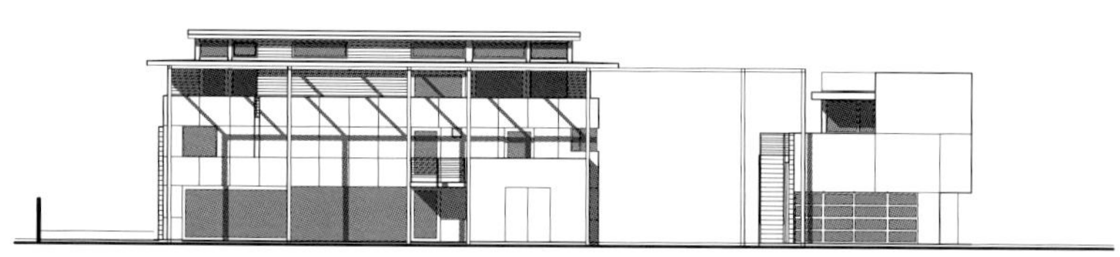

south elevation

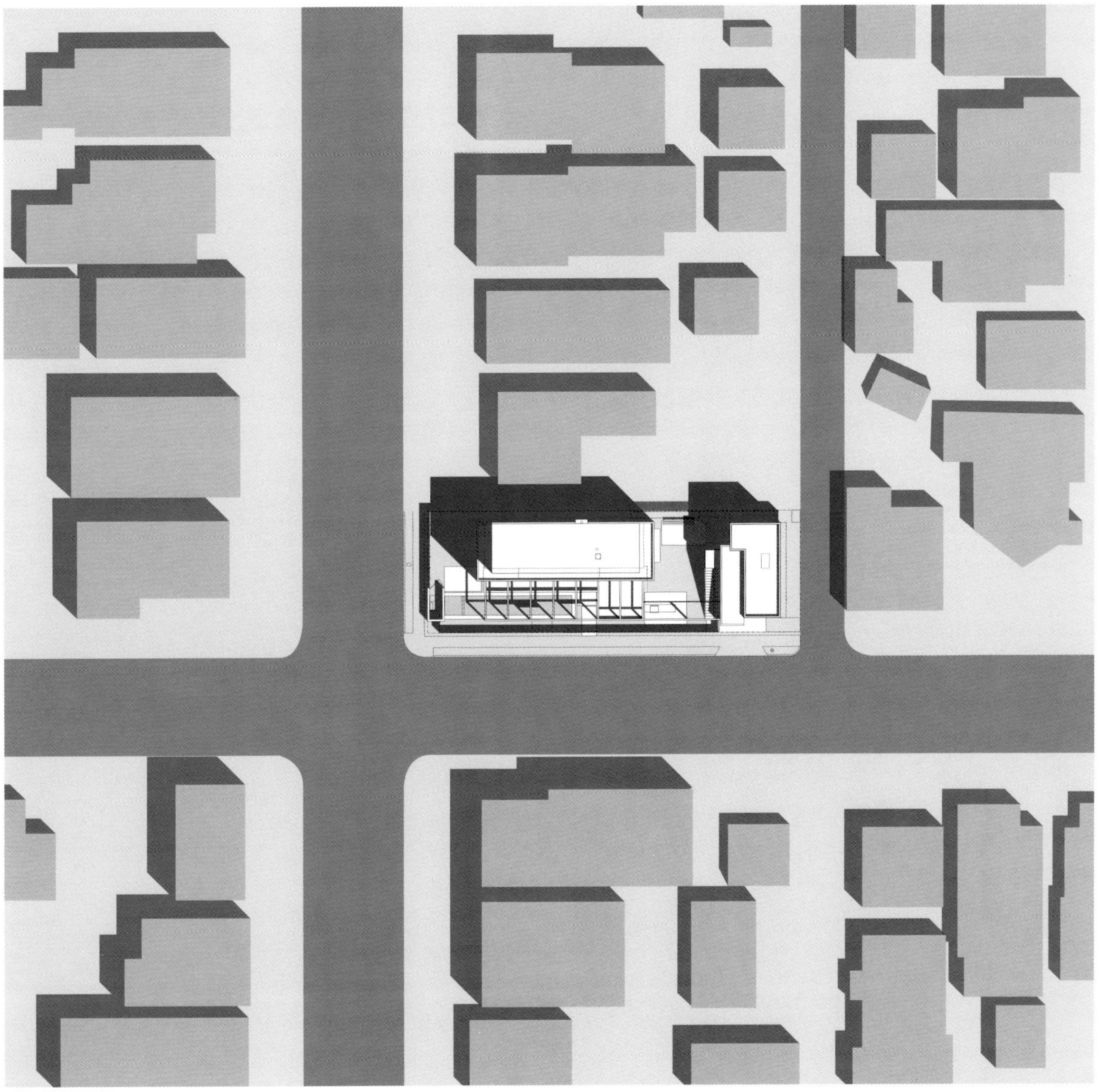

site plan

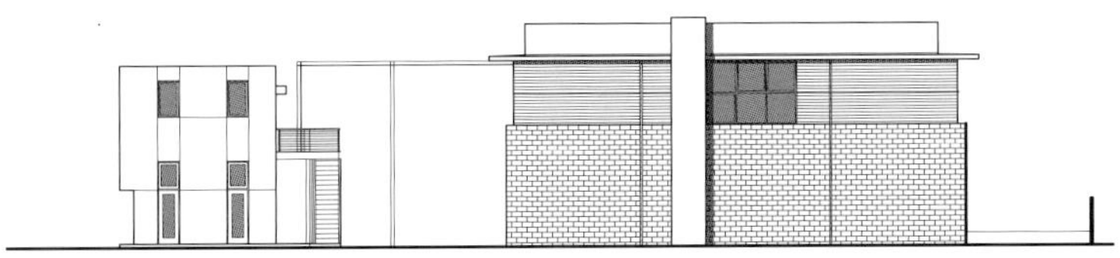

north elevation

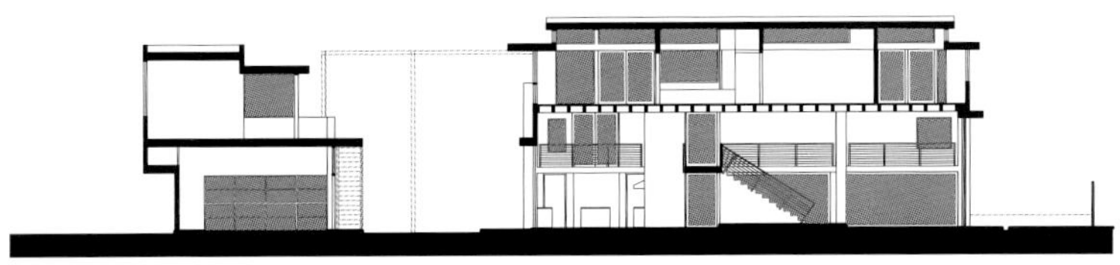

section

700 Palms Residence

Webster Reidence

Venice, California

All year round tourists crowd the Venice boardwalk, gawking at the human carnival of street performers, body builders, and fortunetellers. Just two blocks away, on a walk street closed to cars is the Webster residence. Built for a young professional couple, the Webster house epitomizes the logic of courtyard living within dense, noisy neighborhoods. Its owners can step out and join the funky beach scene in less than a minute, or retreat from the hubbub in their tranquil home with its roof terrace overlooking the Pacific.

This is a savvy split-level that makes the most of limited space and modest materials. The main living spaces are contained in two two-story stucco boxes linked by a garden, with a service core that runs the length of the house on one side. At the front, the living-dining area occupies the ground floor with the master bedroom above, while the rear studio, which is built on a higher level, accommodates a media room on the ground floor and a guest bedroom above.

The imaginative modulation of space, with multiple terraces and vantage points, makes it feel expansive. In its gregarious mode, the house embraces the outdoors with three glass roll-up doors, two that face the interior courtyard and one at the front entrance. The open axis creates uninterrupted views and flowing space from the entrance court through the living-dining area, across the garden and up the stairs to the back studio. Concrete steps ascend to the rear space, providing incidental seating that encourages lingering amid lush plantings and a reflecting pool.

Seeming to float within the service core is a system of steel-grate bridges and stairs, bathed in light from a two-story window wall, that eventually leads to the roof terrace. Exposed structural steel elements and pre-cut concrete panels, chosen for their low cost and durability in the salt air, impart a loft-like ambience. The concrete structural slab is polished and does double-duty as finished flooring. Tucked underneath the elevated rear studio is a two-car garage—a luxury in this beach community where parking is at a premium.

Webster Residence

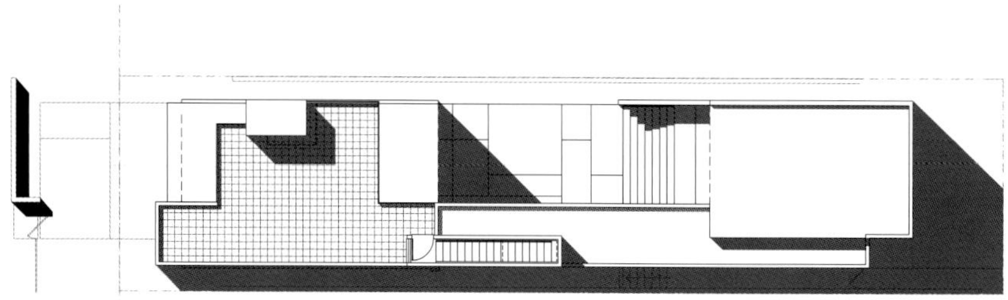

roof plan

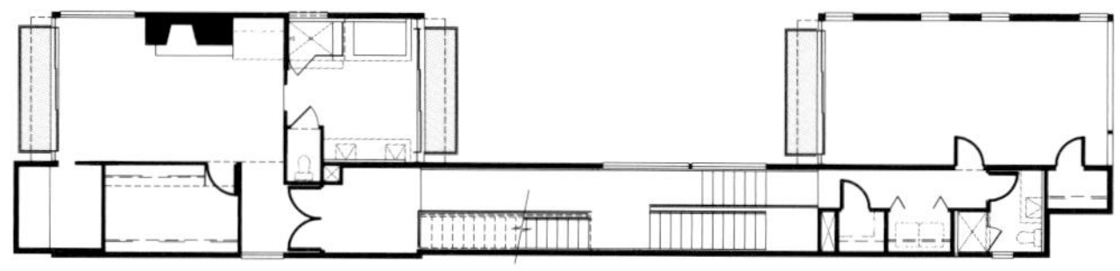

second floor plan

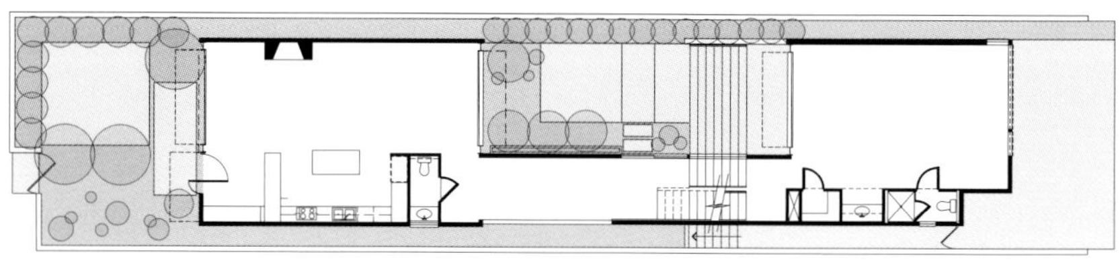

first floor plan

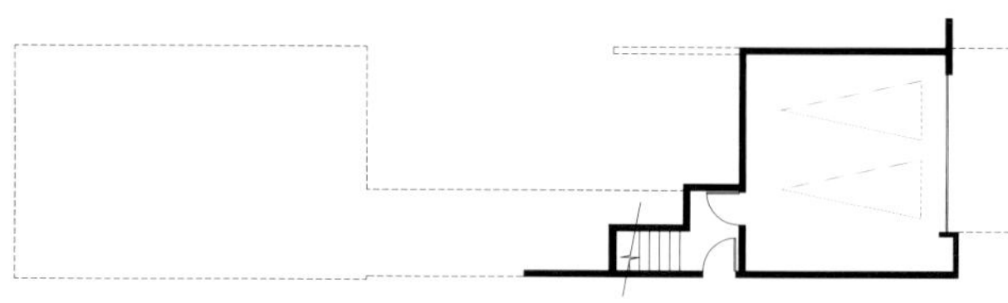

lower level plan

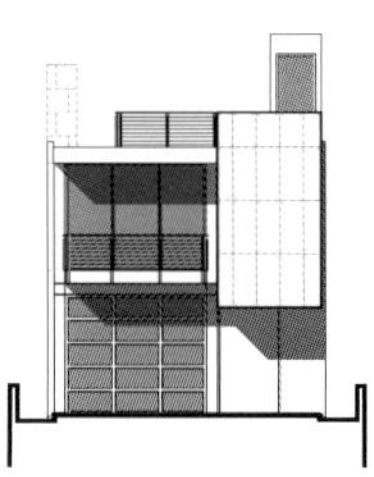

east elevation

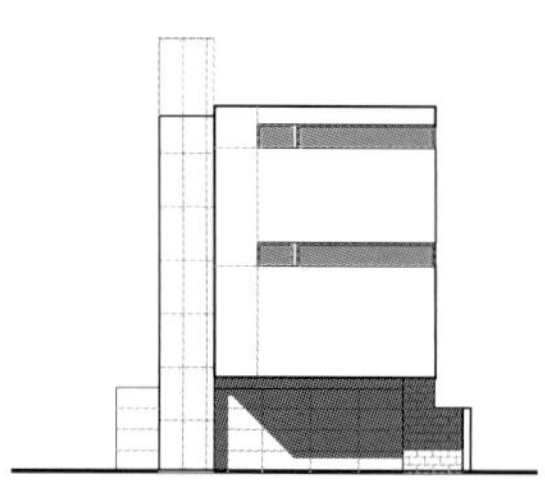

west elevation

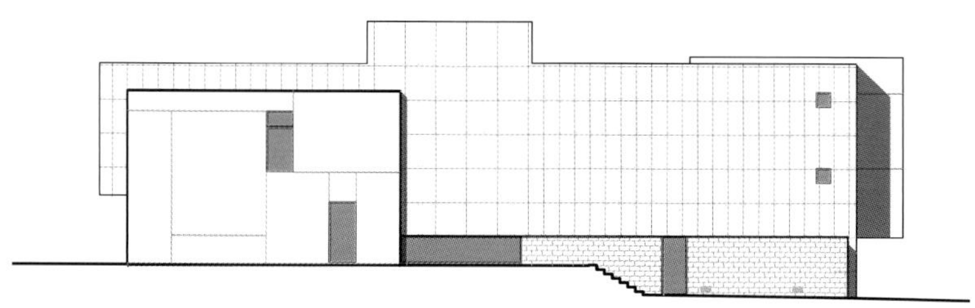

north elevation

site plan

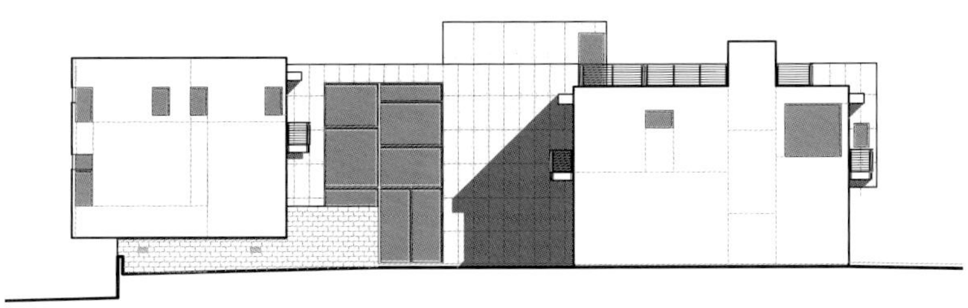

south elevation

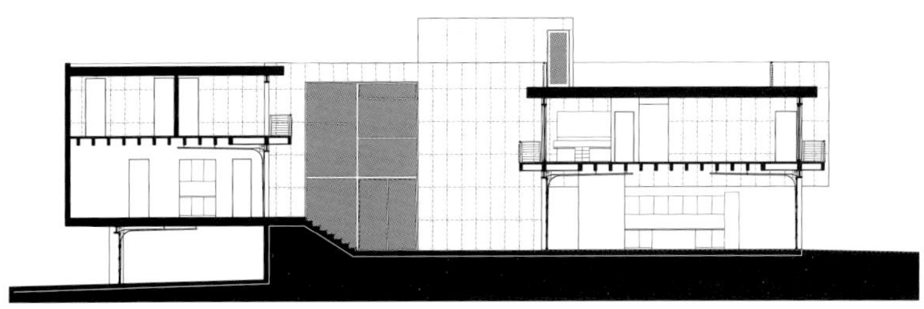

section

Webster Residence

African Forms
Marc Ginzberg
African Forms

Webster Residence

Boxenbaum Residence

Boxenbaum Residence

Beverly Hills, California

A real estate executive and his artist wife, collectors of midcentury furniture, had long nurtured an affinity for modernist architecture. When they decided to build a new home within walking distance of downtown Beverly Hills, a key aspect of their program was the need for generous studio and display space for the resident painter's large canvases. Enthusiastic cooks and hosts, they also wanted kitchen and dining areas suitable for indoor and outdoor entertaining.

The architects were challenged to create an oasis of quiet and privacy on the corner of a busy intersection with an elementary school across the street. Ehrlich and Yanai made a pivotal early design decision to elevate the house, literally and spiritually. By lifting the main floor a half level above ground on the sloping site, it became possible to build a semi-underground basement encompassing a three-car garage, housekeeper's quarters, and storage, all accessed from the lower-grade side street. The basement floor provided an insulating barrier against noise. And with the service functions tucked below, the main floor could be dedicated entirely to gracious living, opening to landscaped gardens on every side.

A limestone staircase of floating planes meanders through the front courtyard and ascends to the main entrance. Inside, the procession continues along a ten-foot wide gallery with walls for hanging art; on the right side of the hallway are living and dining areas, on the left a guest bedroom and study with a hidden Japanese garden, and the master suite. The kitchen and family room at the back of the house, sun-drenched by floor-to-ceiling sliding glass doors, connect to a built-in barbecue and dining patio, sheltered by a roof canopy. Stone stairs and platforms descend through the rear gardens to a reflecting pool with stone sculptures.

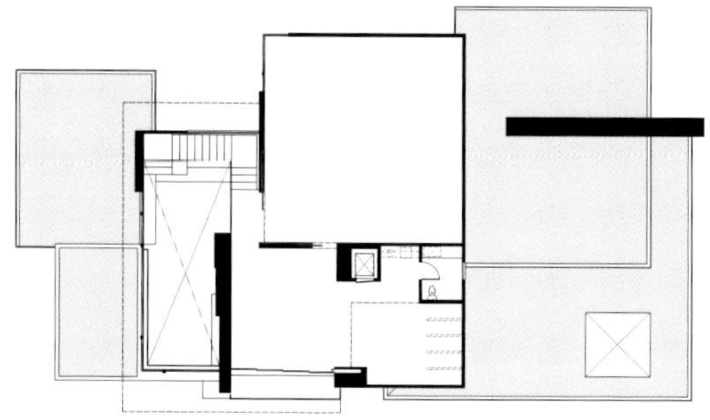

second floor plan

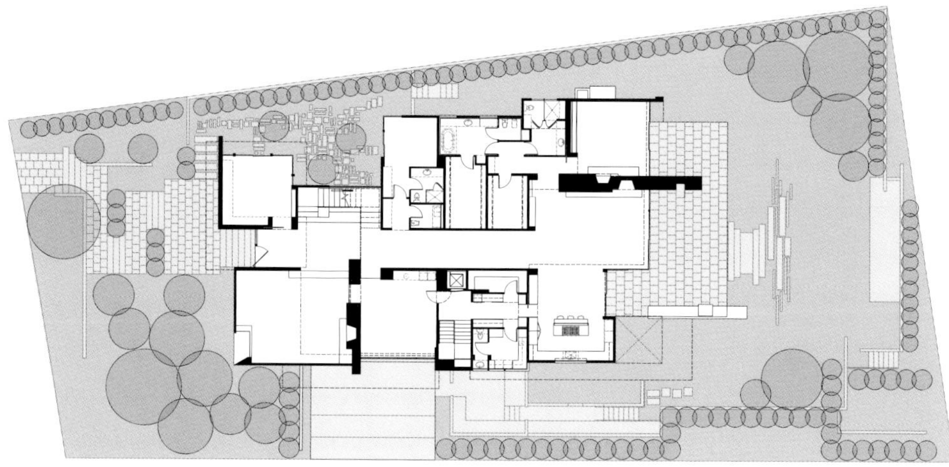

first floor plan

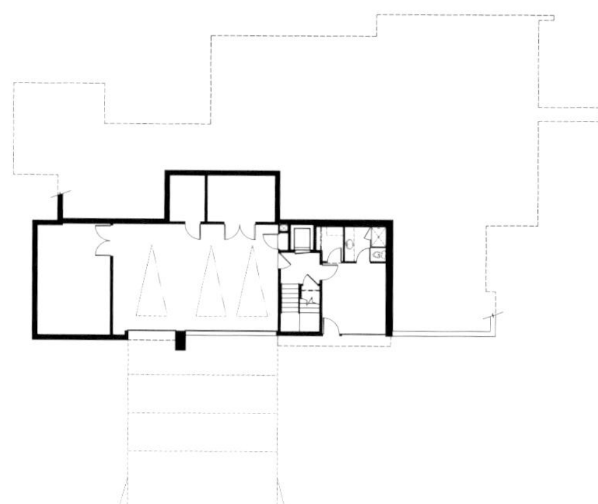

lower level plan

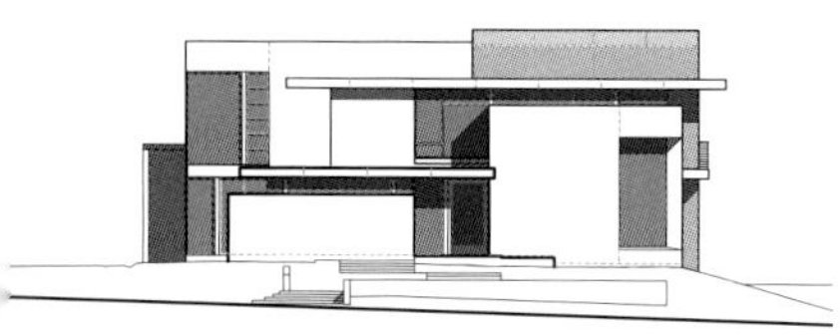

west elevation

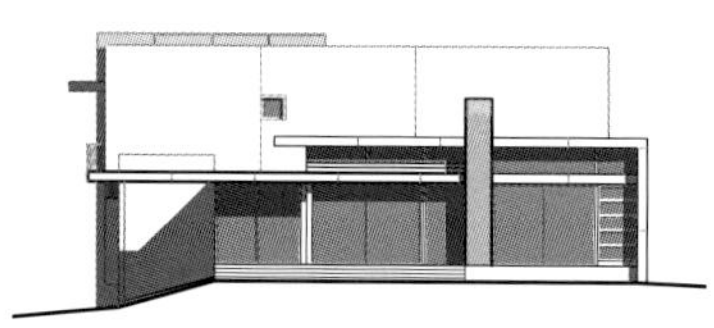

east elevation

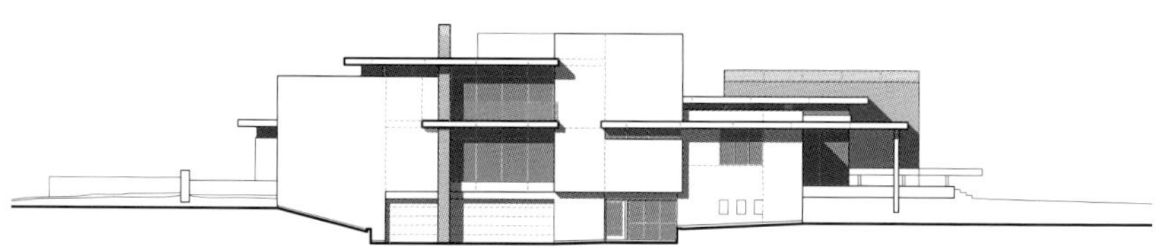

south elevation

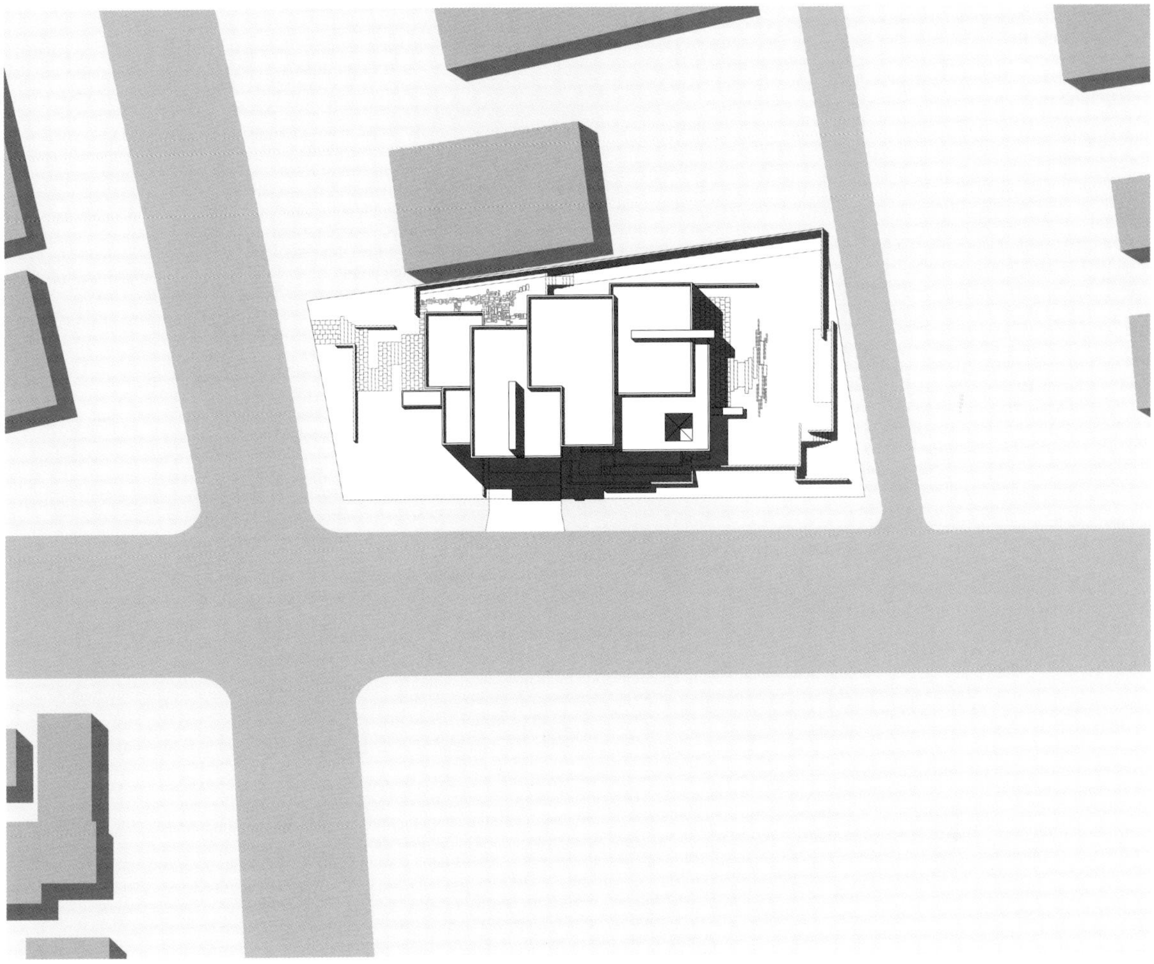

site plan

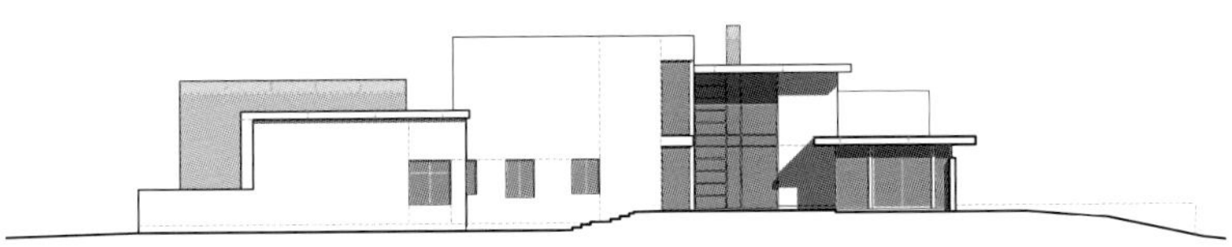

north elevation

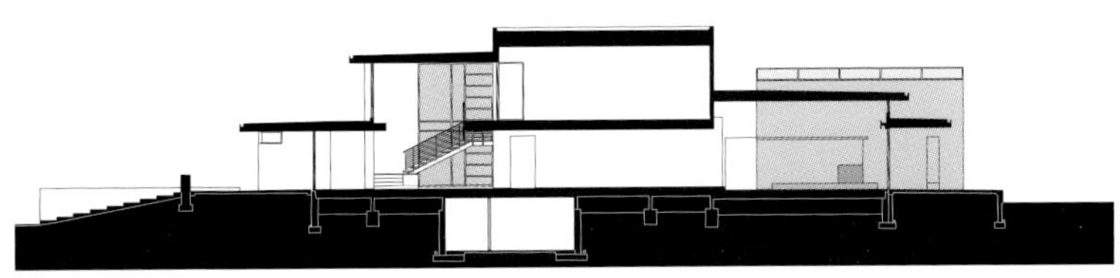

section

The form of the house balances cubic volumes, horizontal roof planes, and vertical stucco masses. The thick gray stucco walls pierce the interior to create sculptural backdrops for fireplaces and extend past glass walls onto the back patio. In the interior, floating stairs of wood and steel lead up to the painting studio, which is finished with tough commercial maple flooring, track lighting, and a corner glass window that admits ambient northern light.

The palette throughout the house is neutral. The custom-finished stucco with its unique troweled texture plays off dark oak and stone floors. Built-in cabinets and bookcases are of walnut. The spaces are designed to showcase modern furniture, including a Mies van der Rohe daybed and chairs in the living room.

Boxenbaum Residence

Boxenbaum Residence

Schulman Residence

Schulman Residence

Brentwood, California

An Oscar-winning screenwriter asked Ehrlich to design a refuge from the stresses of the movie business for himself and his family on a wooded canyon site in Los Angeles. As it happened, Ehrlich had recently returned from working and traveling in Japan, where he had admired ancient building traditions and gardens that foster tranquility. His client's request inspired him to create a home that could be called Zen California Modern, blending crisp geometry and free-flowing space with elegant wood craftsmanship, shoji screens, and contemplative gardens.

Ehrlich's composition lightly places the house in its natural environment, revering the landscape as a wellspring of healing and reflection. The heart of the house is a double-height entrance gallery and living area, flanked by two two-story wings that open to the front and back gardens. The wings enclose family rooms below and bedrooms above. On each side of the entrance are twenty-foot-high, poured-in-place concrete walls that contain two stair towers. A floating bridge joining the two upper floors spans the main volume.

The approach to the house, like the entrance to a Buddhist temple, encourages a mindful transition from the chaos of the outside world to a serene private realm. Modeled on a classic Japanese garden, the forecourt features a wooden footbridge, traditional plantings, large rocks found on the property, a koi pond, and a murmuring waterspill. The parking garage is neatly tucked into a hillside, off to the side and out of sight.

Warm materials and refined details support the East-meets-West aesthetic. Mitered glass corner windows and horizontal wooden mullions evoke the spirit of Frank Lloyd Wright, another architect who admired the Japanese aesthetic. Windows to the entrance court slide back like Asian screens. Rainwater pours down chains instead of downspouts, a Japanese element. A fireplace in the living room is made of polished granite with a bronze mantel. Steel stair rails set off rich wood tones including mahogany floors and maple cabinets. The owners furnished the house with a mix of modern and antique Asian furniture.

Aspects of the Schulman house that are emphatically not Japanese are its dynamic flow of open space and the eighteen-foot height of the living room—bold gestures not found in traditional Asian buildings. Here the American love of drama melds with eastern serenity, achieving a delicate balance.

Schulman Residence

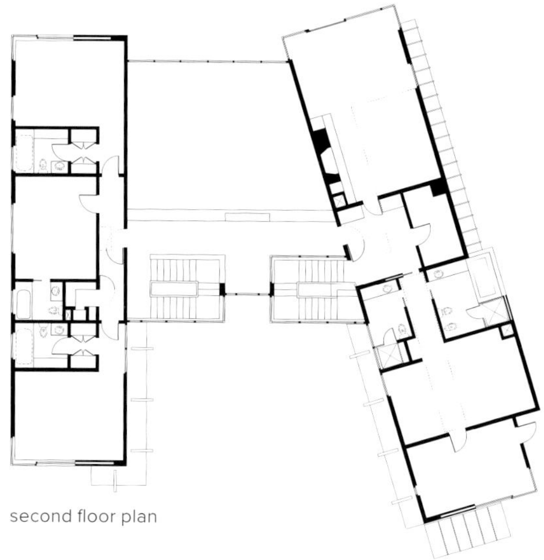

second floor plan

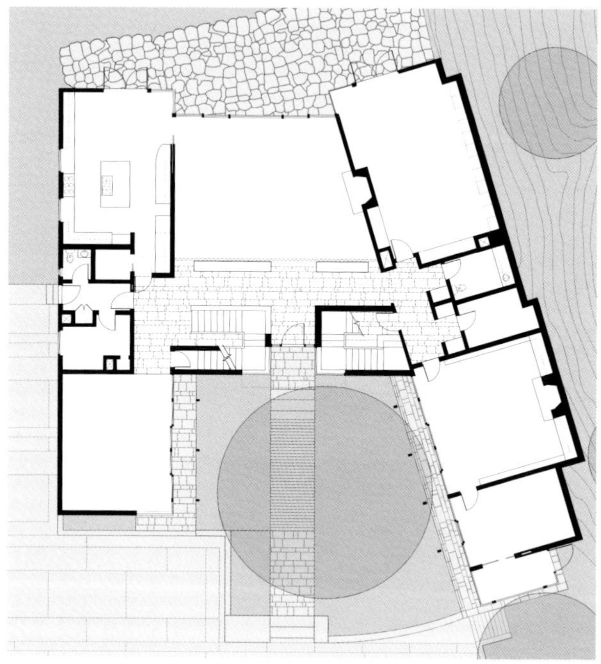

first floor plan

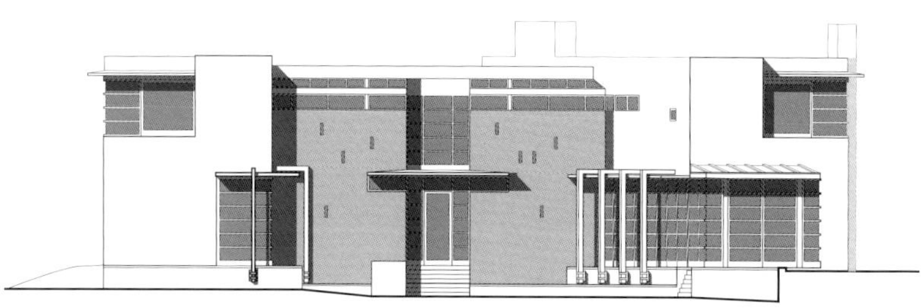

south elevation

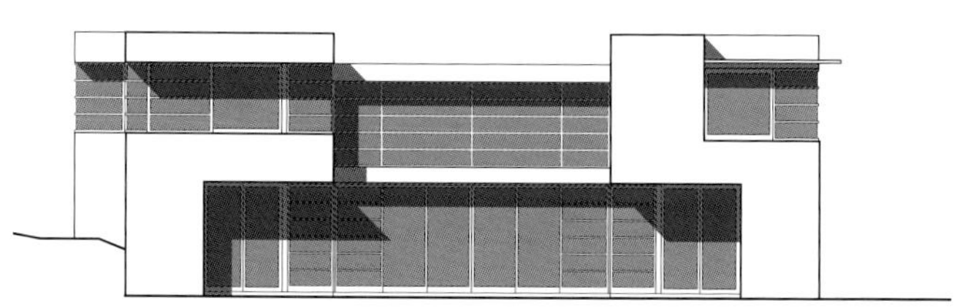

north elevation

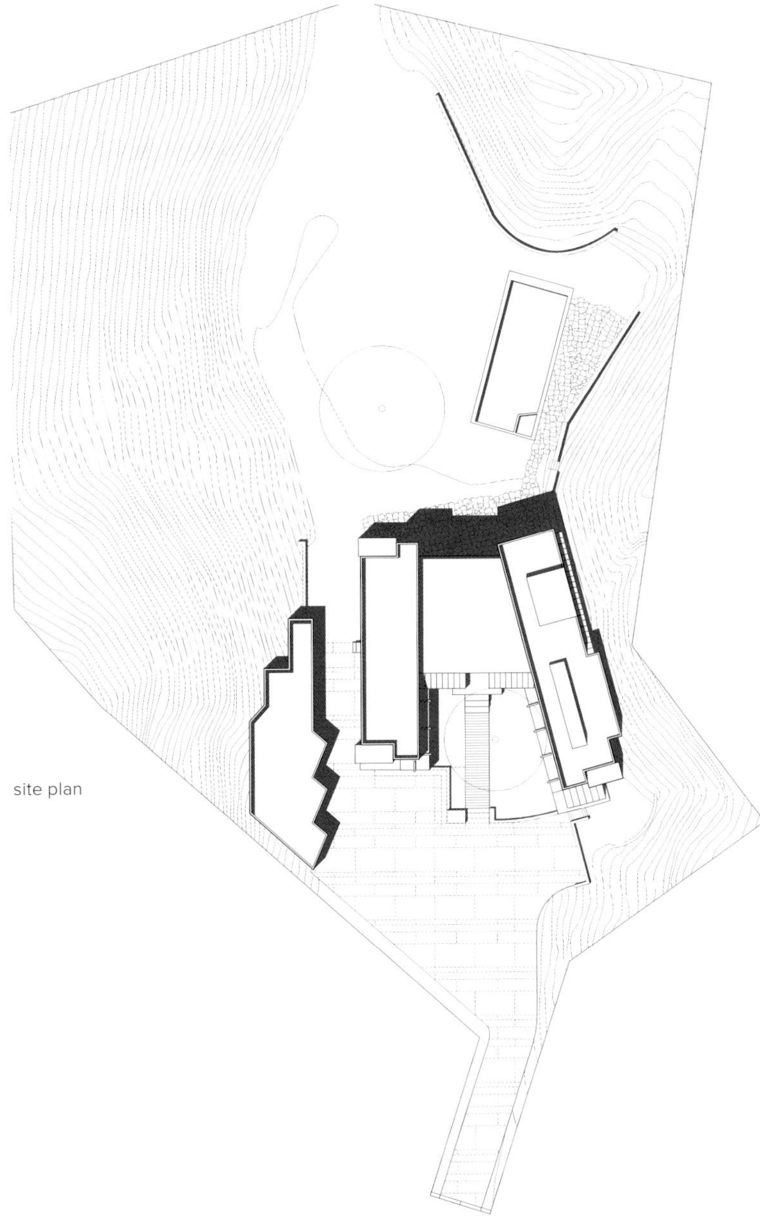

site plan

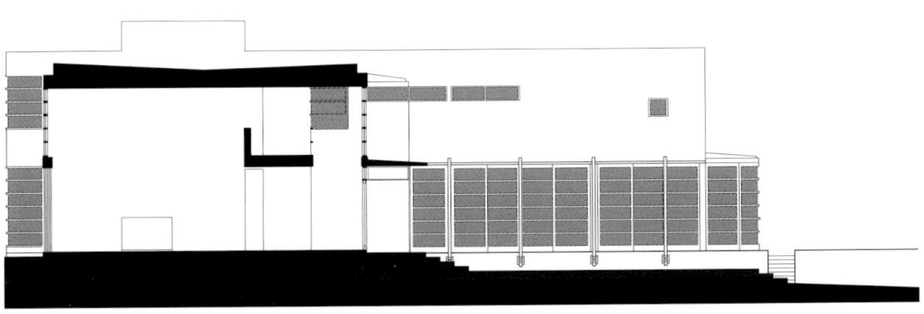

section

Schulman Residence

Schulman Residence

Robert Capa Photographs
Georgia O'Keeffe
Walker Evans First and Last

605

Canyon Residence

Santa Monica, California

This is a house that wants to dance with nature, not dominate it. The Canyon house rambles down its sloping site, dodging fifty-year-old California sycamore trees and cozying up to a spring-fed stream. The choreography of living spaces, outdoor stairs, and floating decks immerses the owners in an intimate and ever-shifting connection to their environment, a Los Angeles canyon of majestic grandeur.

Underlying the house's lively demeanor is a rigorous order. The L-shaped plan separates a double-story living, dining, and kitchen area from the two-story bedroom wing. Ehrlich created a series of vertical masses of custom-colored stucco rhythmically aligned in a north-south formation, housing such elements as fireplaces, stairs, mechanical cores, and storage. Copper-clad canopies constitute a horizontal counterpoint and protect glass windows and wooden doors from rain and sun. The cascade of masses, planes, and steps terminates in an out-of-ground swimming pool, a blue rectangle jutting into the landscape.

Colors and textures indoors and out take their cues from the landscape. Stucco walls were tinted with natural pigments custom-mixed to match the mottled hues found in the bark of the sycamores. The stucco of the double-height living room wall is hand-trowelled and slashed into an expressionistic surface, with irregular-shaped nooks that showcase the owners' collection of Asian artifacts and pottery from Peru, China, and Italy. White stone stair treads emerge from the wall with no visible means of support.

Several varieties of naturally finished wood harmonize with other materials and echo the rustic setting. Douglas fir was used for door and window frames and mullions. The decks are made to last of stalwart ironwood. Indoors, the floors are of Brazillian cherry with touches of Italian marble. Built-in cabinets and wall display shelves are crafted of sycamore, eucalyptus, and cherry.

Canyon Residence

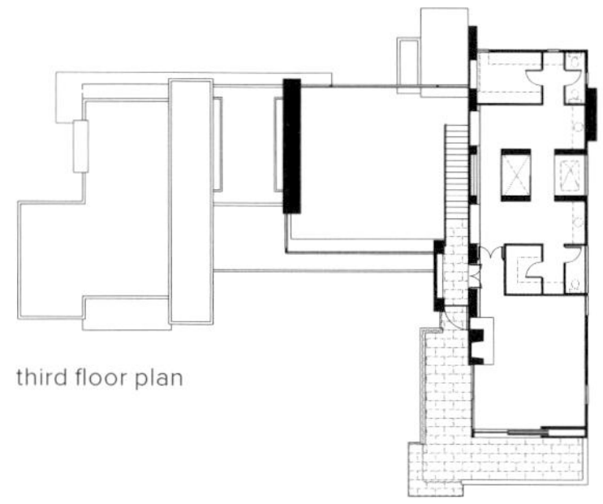
third floor plan

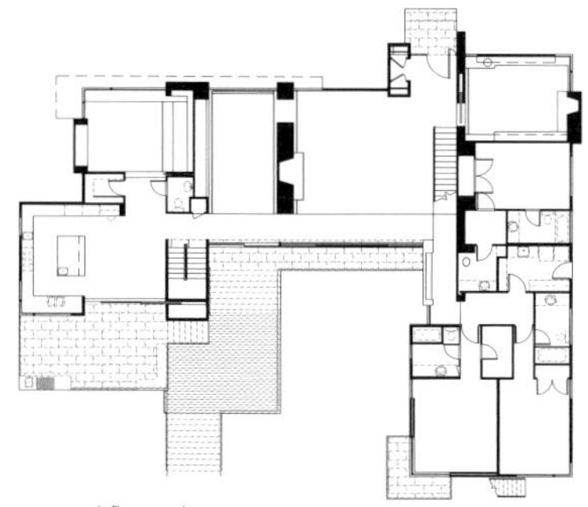
second floor plan

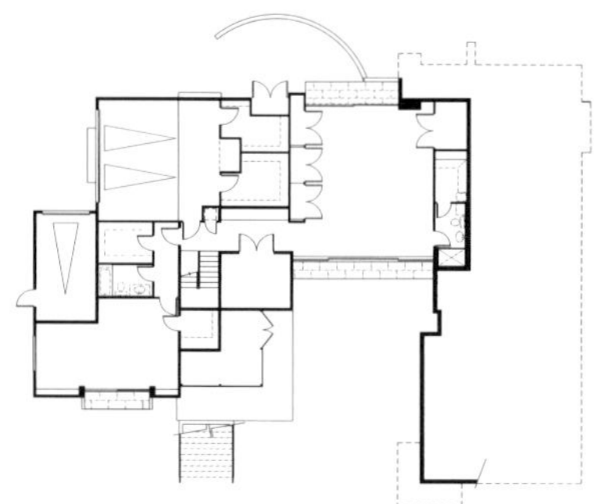
first floor plan

20'/6m

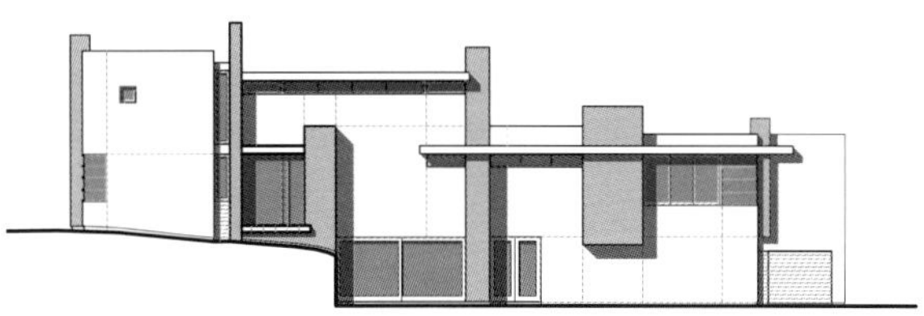
north elevation

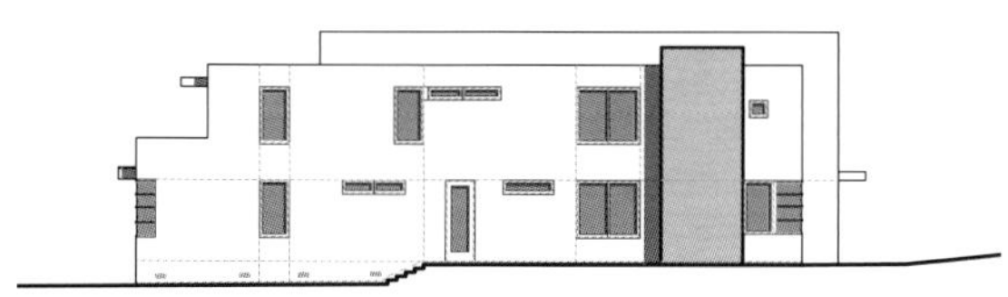
east elevation

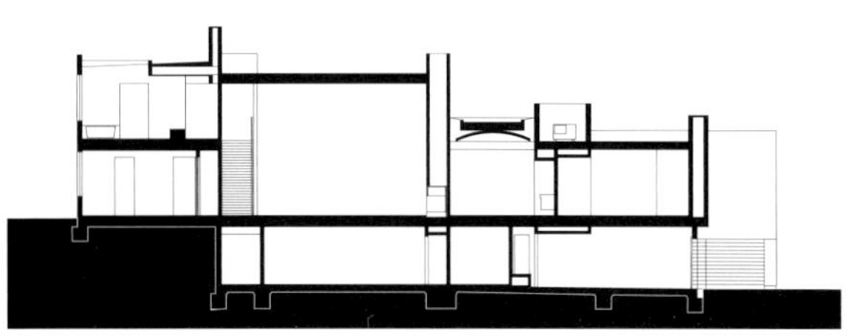
section

site plan

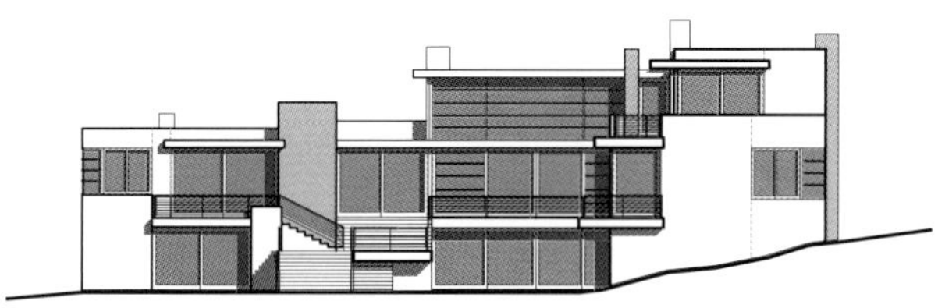

south elevation

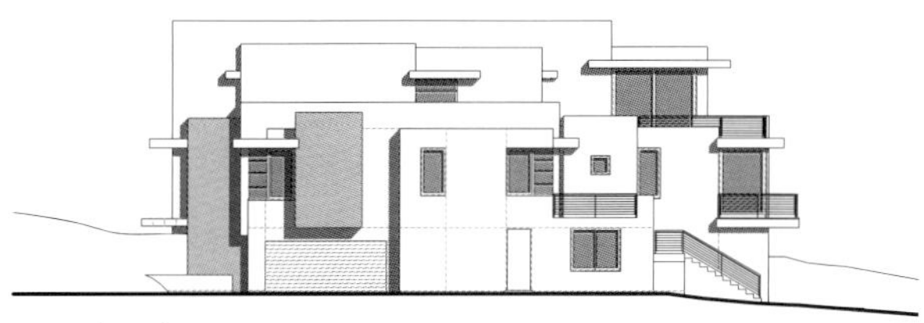

west elevation

Canyon Residence

MOREZ-DU-JURA

Waldfogel Residence

Palo Alto, California

A technology entrepreneur and his wife had talked for years of building a modern house in which to raise their young daughter and display their collection of twentieth-century American art and ceramics. This residence is their sophisticated dream house, utterly contemporary but understated enough to blend unobtrusively into a traditional suburban community a mile from Stanford University. It's a house that expresses itself quietly with the discipline of its lines, splendid materials and finishes, and meticulous attention to detail.

Ehrlich and Yanai organized the house, which occupies a flat site, around a three-foot-thick poured-in-place concrete axial wall. Two parallel two-story wings extend from the central spine, opening to four distinct garden courtyards. A double-height window wall floods a stainless steel and frosted glass staircase with light opposite the dining area. The stair continues down to a 3,000 square-foot finished basement, which accommodates a recreation area, exercise room, gallery space, and laundry, built underground because Palo Alto building codes limit on above-ground building; a benefit of this strategy was increased space for gardens.

The stucco facades are tautly opposed by horizontal overhanging roofs of Rheinzink, a naturally weathering matte-finish metal that reflects soft light back into the interiors. Mitred glass corners frame unobstructed garden views. The kitchen and family room courtyard includes a swimming pool, while the owner's study looks out onto a garden with two mature cedar trees. The connection of indoor to outdoor space is reinforced throughout the house by sliding doors and windows, and limestone floors that extend into courts as hardscape.

The monolithic concrete spine that bisects the house is crafted with a surface as silky as marble. As it passes through living areas, this wall is punctuated by shelves displaying ceramics, or backrests for built-in banquettes. Throughout the house dark-red mahogany panels and trims applied in Mondrianesque patterns offset the coolness of the concrete. Fireplaces are also built of cast concrete, while floors are stone or walnut.

The house serves as a private gallery for the owners' carefully chosen furniture and works of art, including a yellow Robert Motherwell painting that hangs above a yellow couch in the living room, and an Antony Gormley sculpture on the hearth.

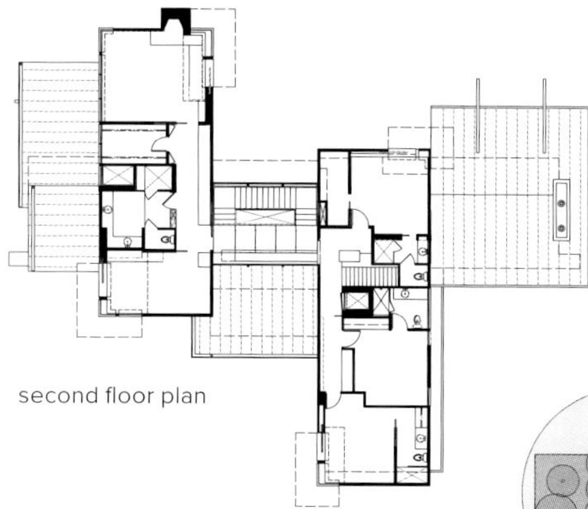

second floor plan

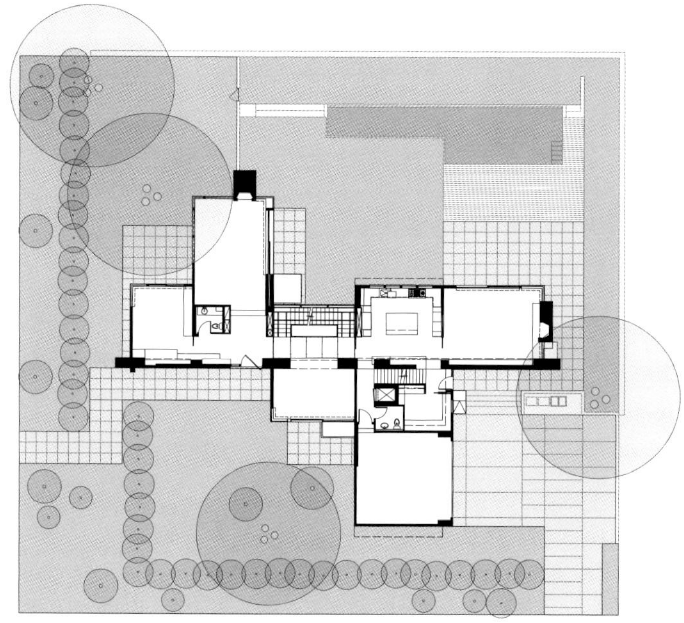

first floor plan

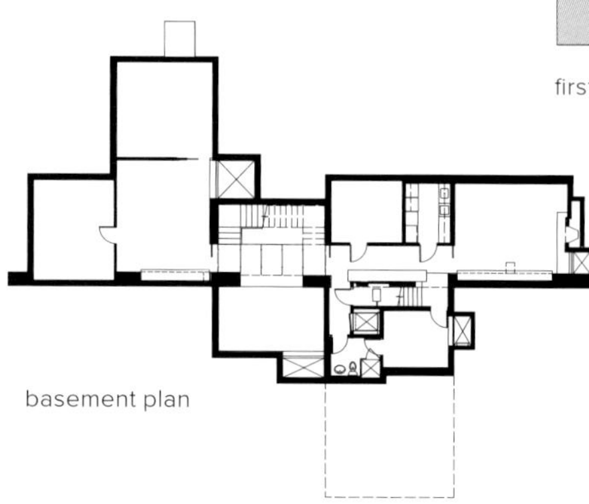

basement plan

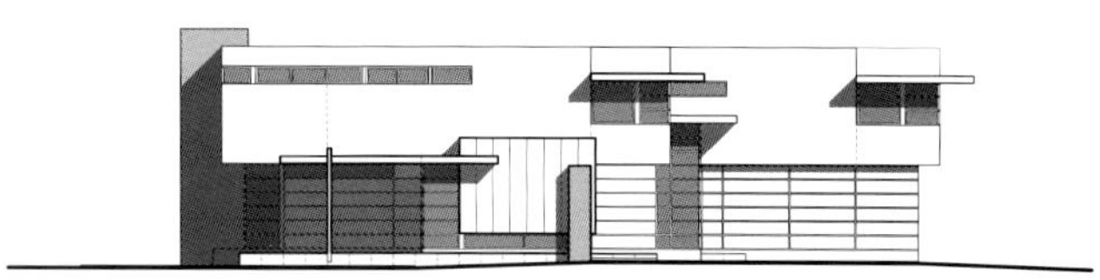

south elevation

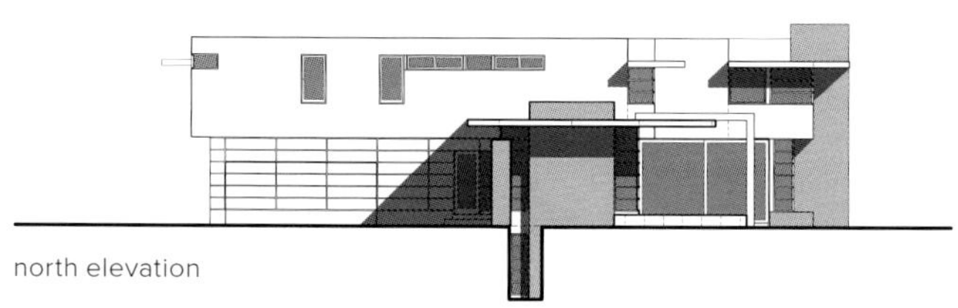

north elevation

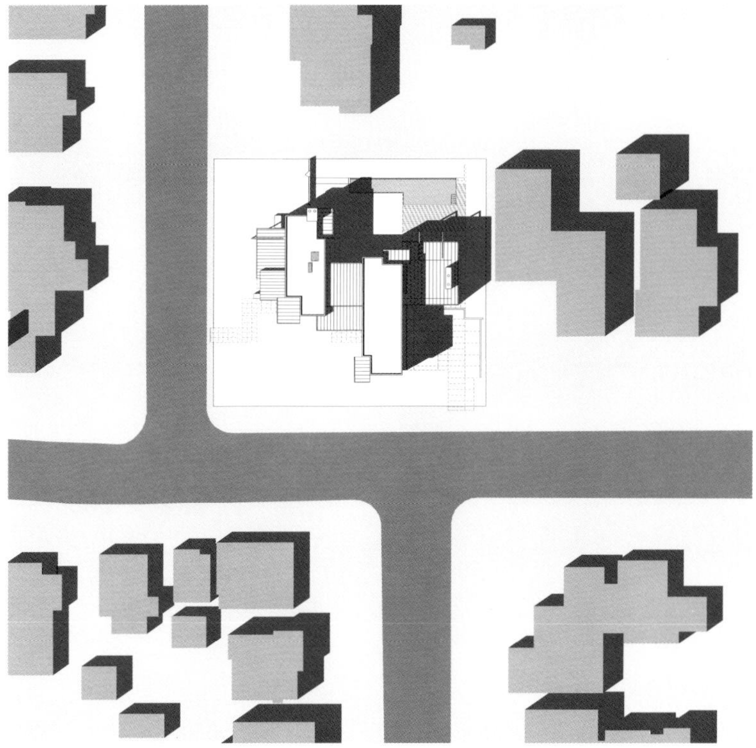
site plan

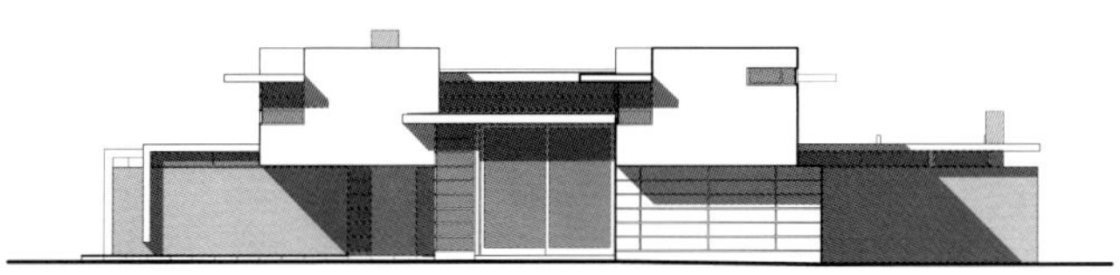
east elevation

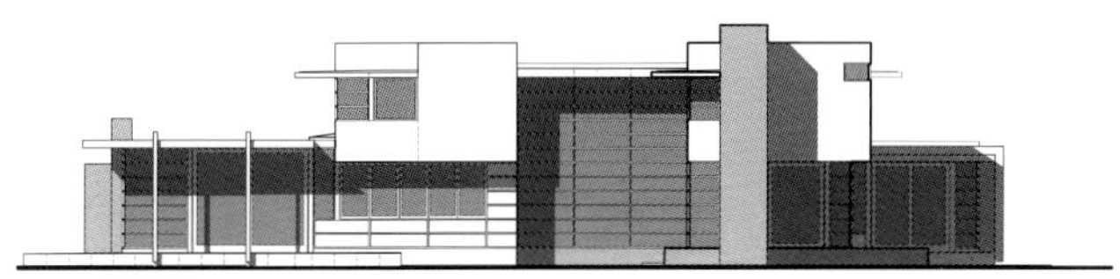
west elevation

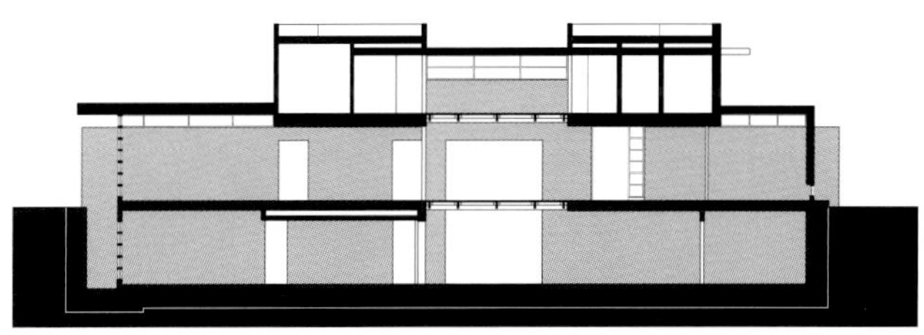
section

Waldfogel Residence

Waldfogel Residence

Waldfogel Residence

451

Zeidler Residence

Aptos, California

Like a kind of coastal chameleon, this house absorbs and reflects the ever-changing colors and moods of its site on a bluff overlooking the Pacific Ocean. Built for a couple with grown children, the Zeidler residence is a casual but gracious platform for living by the sea, offering myriad places to savor the sunshine, breezes, and views.

Ehrlich and Yanai designed the house as two buildings that appear to be clusters of cubes, like children's blocks, separated by a courtyard. They chose contrasting exterior materials to break up the sculptural volumes with a rich interplay of textures, and to weather in the salt air. Exposed concrete block and troweled stucco are juxtaposed with Rheinzinc, a durable metal that acquires a shimmering luster over time. Cast glass screens at the front entrance and a corner of the pool capture light and seem to emanate a translucent glow.

The primary living spaces are contained in the two-and-one-half story main house. The ground floor is an open plan with a double-height living room, dining area, and kitchen, all with unobstructed views of the ocean and generous walls for displaying the clients' California modern art collection. When separation is desired, the living room can be closed off with a frosted glass pocket door that disappears into the wall. The owners, wine-lovers who spend part of the year in France, keep a wine cellar and tasting area in the full basement.

A walnut and stainless-steel staircase leads up to the master wing with its balcony and panoramic view, then up another flight to a roof deck. Equipped with a built-in barbecue, outdoor kitchen, and burnished concrete block fireplace, the roof is a favorite spot for enjoying the sunset with a glass of champagne. An elevator serves every level of the house and facilitates entertaining.

Tall sliding glass doors connect the house to nature. The inner courtyard has a lap pool and hardscaping for displaying outdoor sculptures. With its own full barbecue and food serving area, it offers an alternative for al fresco dining. In the front courtyard is a petanque court for outdoor bowling, a passion the couple acquired in France.

The guesthouse at the back of the property encompasses three private living quarters for frequent visits from relatives and friends, as well as a garage. The second-floor studio has a full kitchen and its own deck with impressive ocean views.

450

Zeidler Residence

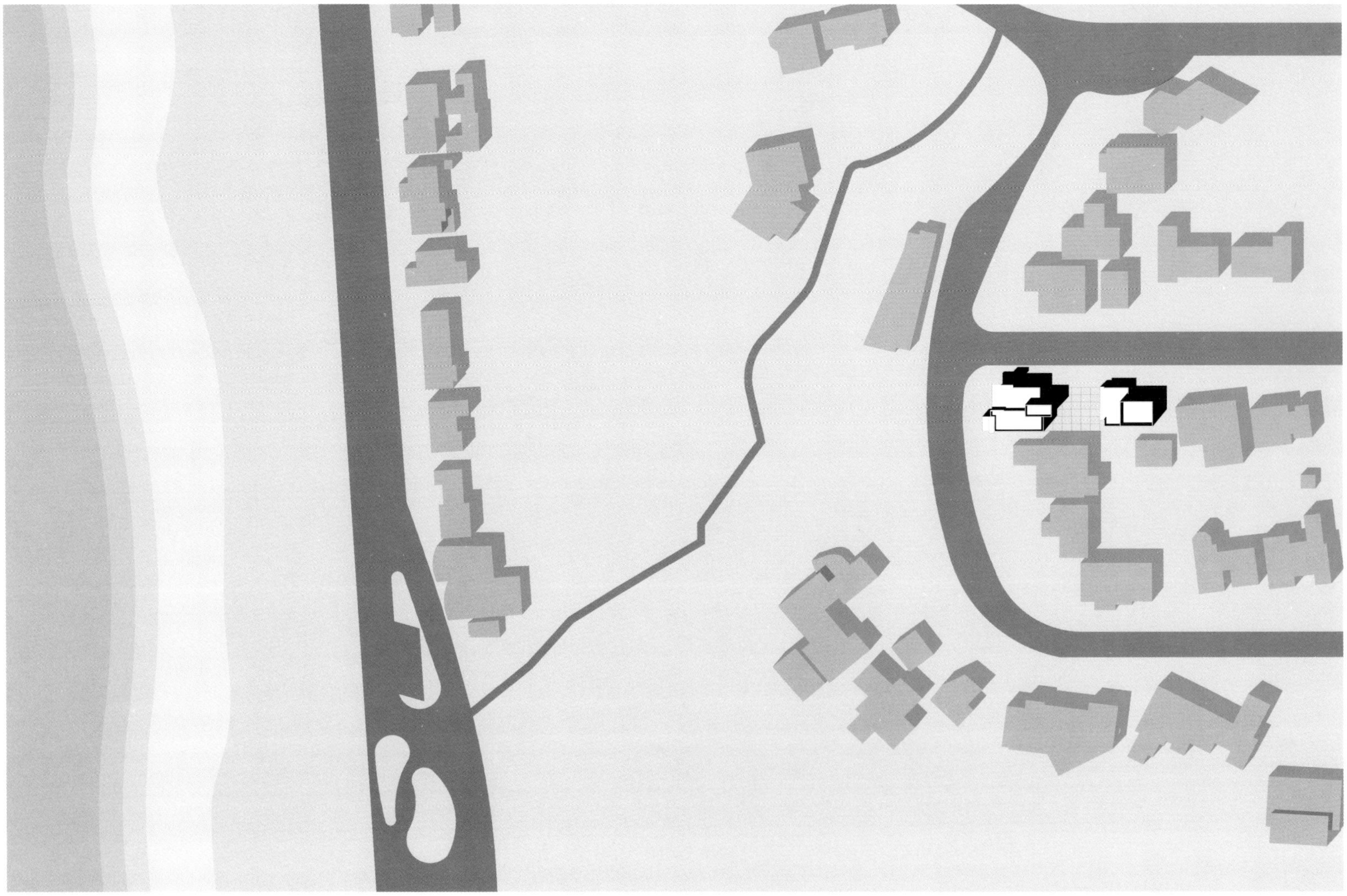

site plan

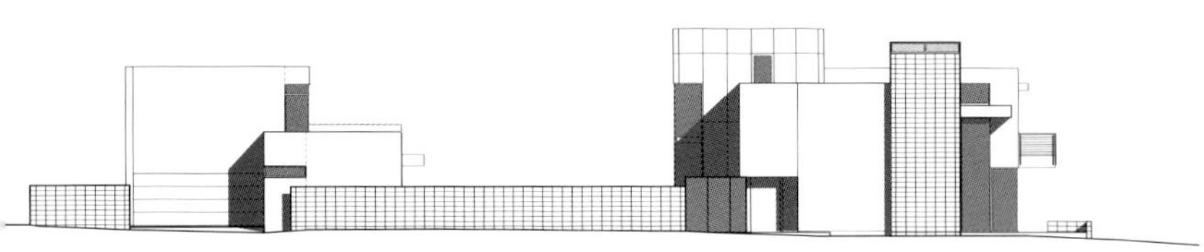

north elevation

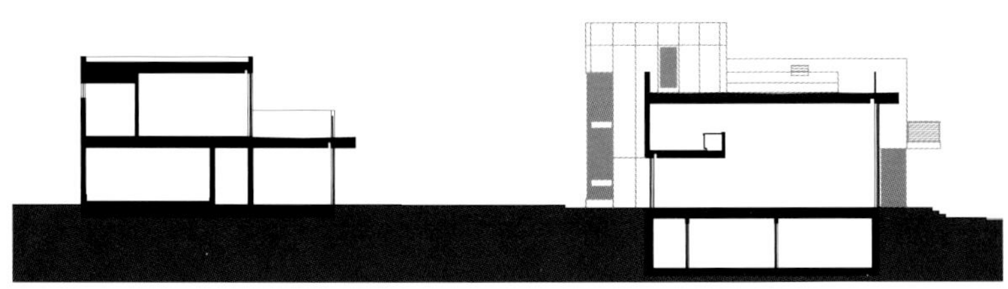

section

Zeidler Residence

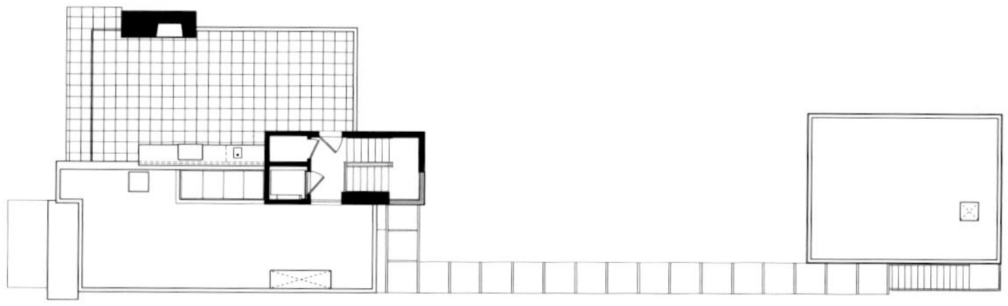

third floor plan

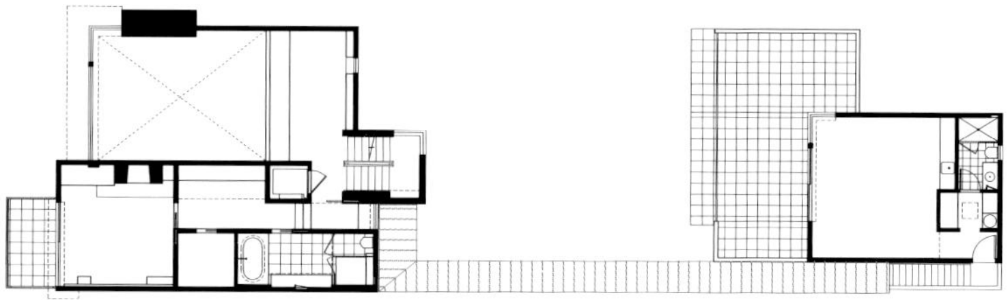

second floor plan

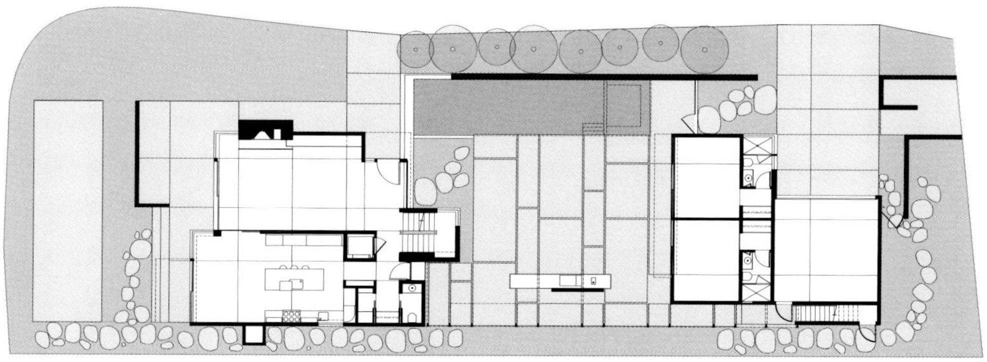

first floor plan

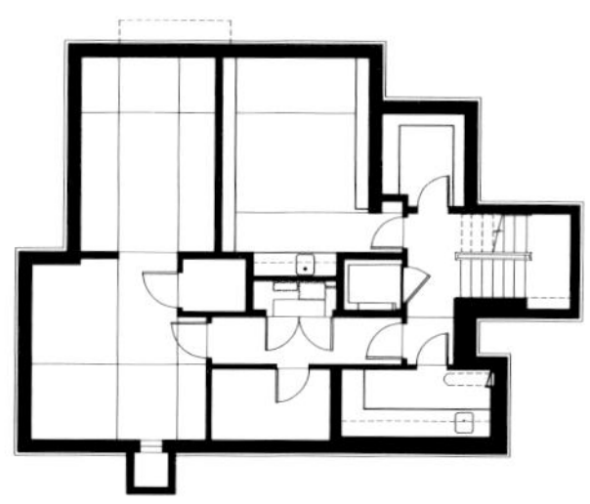

basement plan

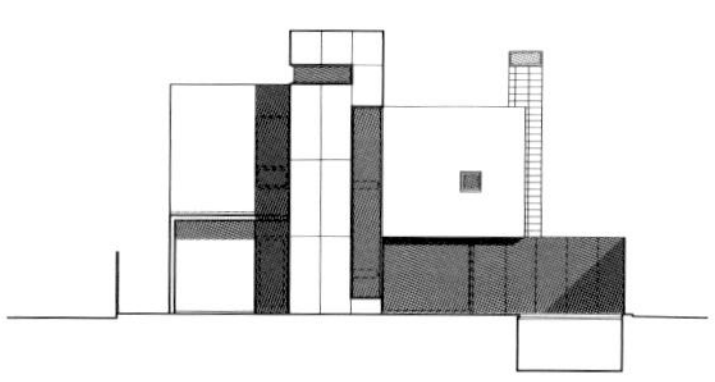

northeast elevation

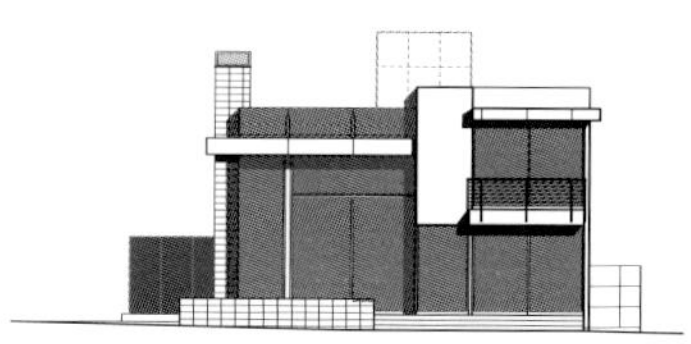

southwest elevation

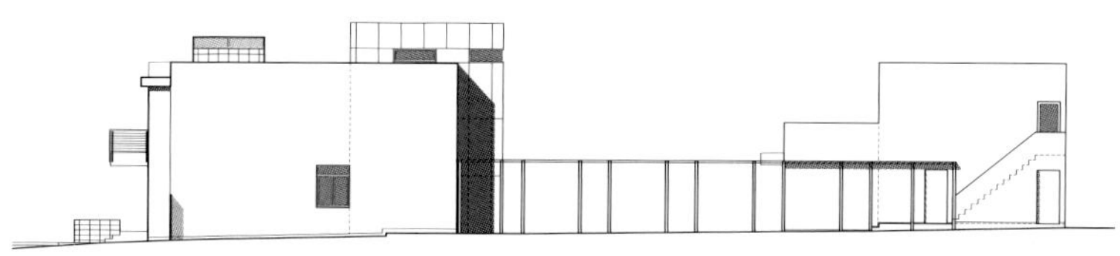

southeast elevation

JULIUS SHUL
MODERNIS

Zeidler Residence

Zeidler Residence

Leonard Residence

Leonard Residence

Los Angeles, California

Steep hillsides studded with homes that cling to them, defying gravity, attest to the fact that a certain breed of Los Angeles canyon-dweller cannot resist a great view. The owners of this house fit squarely into that category, willing to undertake the difficulties of building on a precipitous site in order to gaze out over the Los Angeles basin at night, a carpet of twinkling lights at their feet. The couple decided the time was right to demolish their 1940s-era Hollywood hillside home and rebuild when they were living temporarily in New York. The site offered a classic sweeping vista, with snow-capped mountains to the east and the blue waters of the Pacific to the west.

Ehrlich's dilemma was to maximize the spectacular views while insuring privacy from nearby neighbors, and meet a program for living and working within a small footprint. The design solution, a three-story wall of glass supported by steel and concrete, with outdoor decks at every level, is an homage to the famous Case Study houses of Los Angeles. A two-story living room is suspended over the canyon on a structured concrete slab that also serves as the finished floor. Mitred glass at one corner allows for an unimpeded view, while windows and walls are all strategically placed to insure privacy, editing views both in and out.

From the main level, a floating tread stair ascends to the master suite with his-and-hers bathooms and access to a large secluded roof deck above the garage. The lower level, reached by a stair anchored to a cast-in-place concrete wall, includes home office and guest quarters with the same astounding views.

Efficient use of space permitted a small landscaped courtyard terrace on the ground level near the front entrance. The concrete slab helps cool the house in summer and conserve heat in winter. Adding a rustic touch to the abundance of concrete and glass is earth-colored stucco for exterior walls and warm wood cabinetry indoors. The dining room features a permanently installed Cor-Ten steel-and-glass table designed by the architects.

Leonard Residence

Leonard Residence

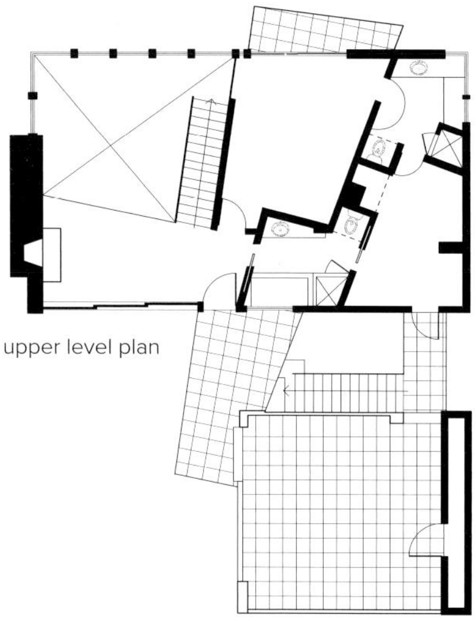

upper level plan

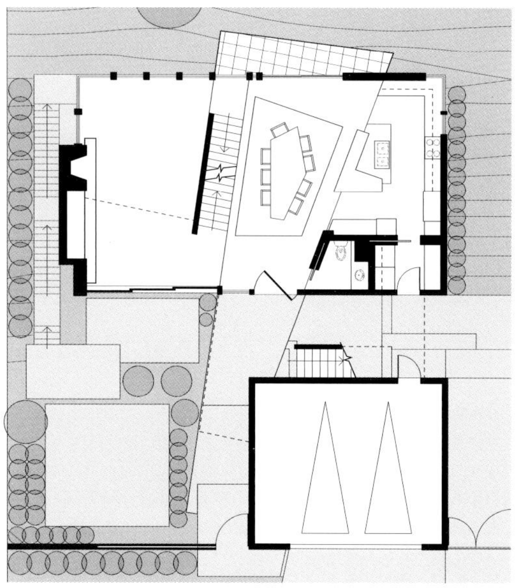

main level plan

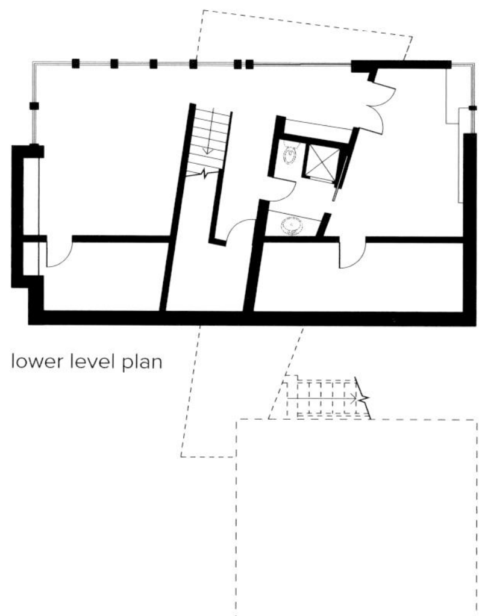

lower level plan

10'/3m

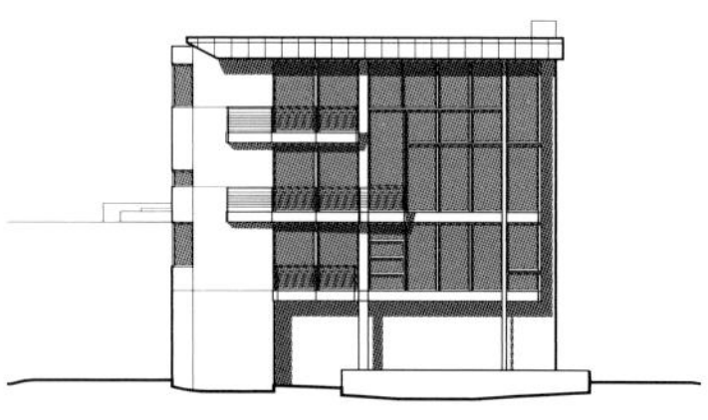

south elevation

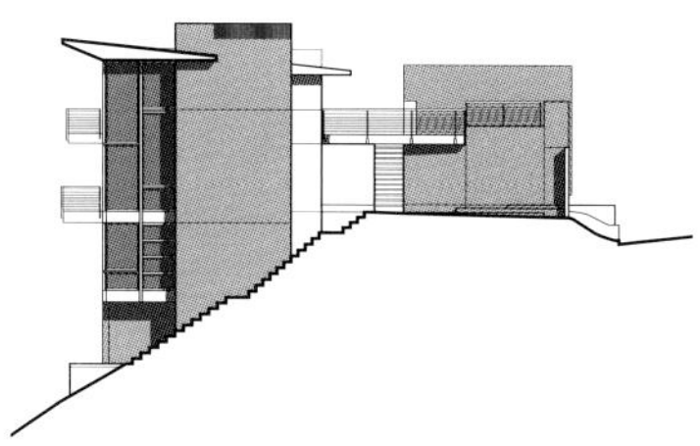

east elevation

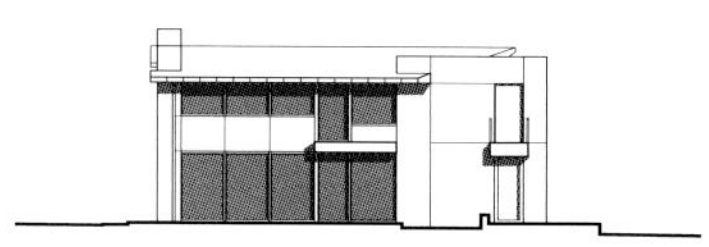

north elevation

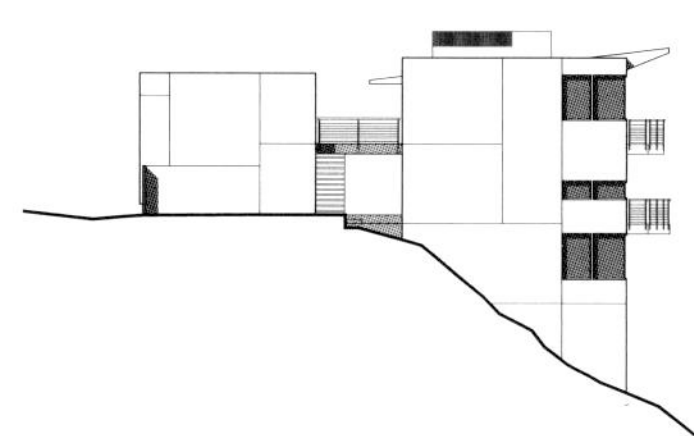

west elevation

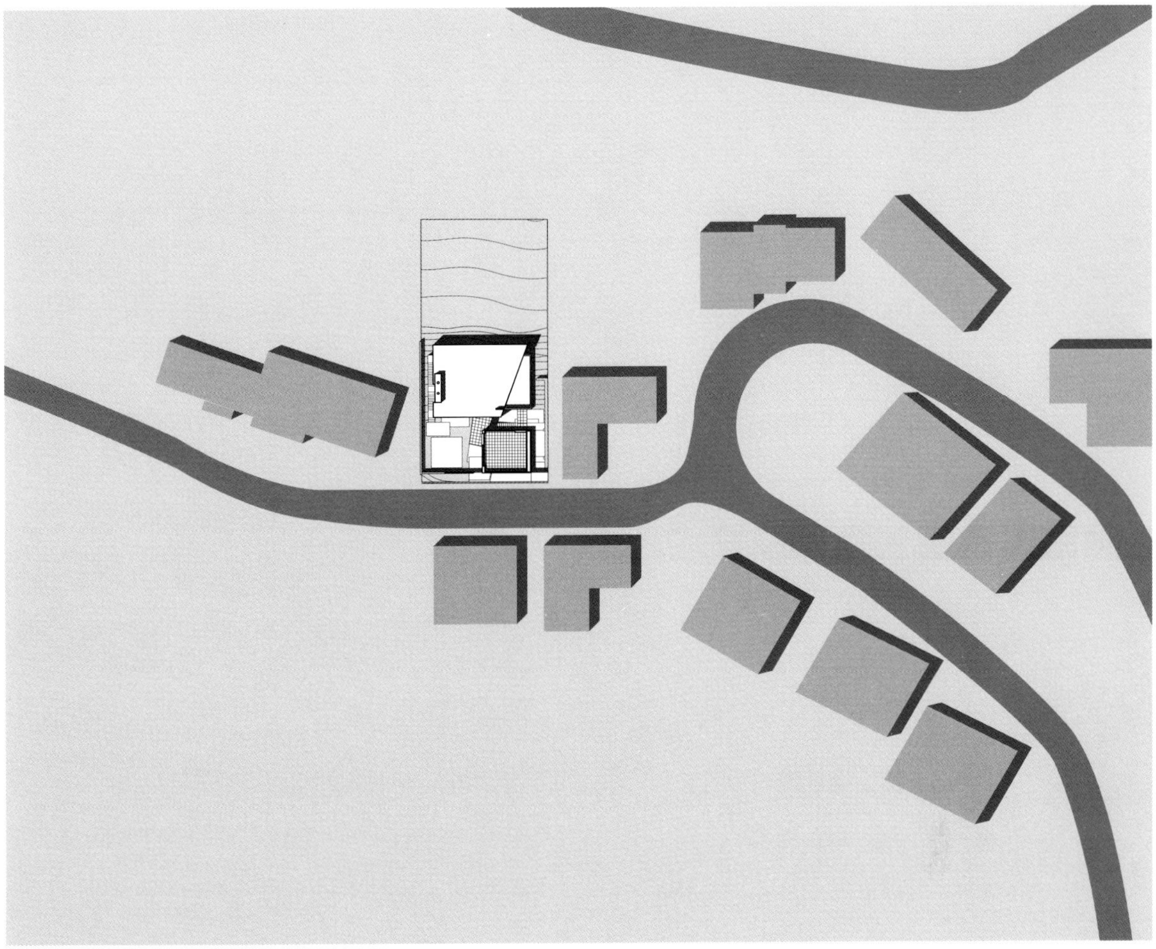

site plan

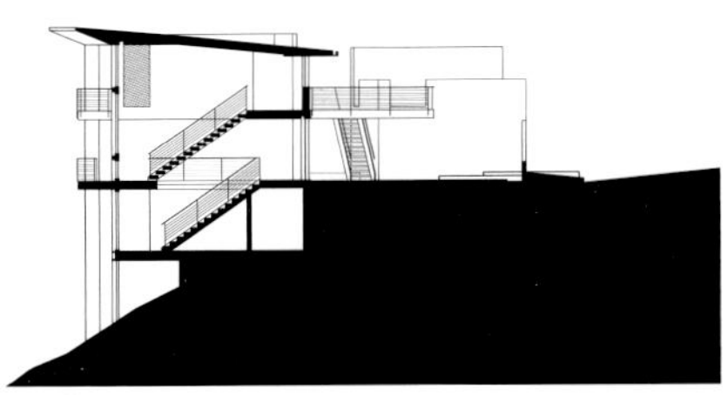

section

Leonard Residence

Leonard Residence

Carrillo Residence

Carrillo Residence

Pacific Palisades, California

The property's dramatic views clinched the deal, persuading a professional couple with two young boys to purchase a long, narrow slice of land on the rim of Santa Monica Canyon. The clients asked Ehrlich and Yanai to design a home balancing areas for formal adult entertaining with those catering to the daily needs of family life. They envisioned a palette of neutral colors with a soothing ambience. And of course the house should make the most of its mesmerizing views of the wooded canyon it overlooks and the Pacific Ocean in the distance.

The architects devised a simple elongated plan that reinforces the geometry of the site. The ground floor is defined by four thick limestone walls that impart mass and texture. The upper story bedroom wings are housed in a white stucco box that slides past the stone base, as if reaching for the view.

A glass living pavilion sits at the far end of the site perpendicular to the main space and adjacent to the formal dining area. This glass volume, anchored by a stone wall, divides the grounds into two distinct courtyards. Family areas at floor level open out to an informal inner garden, providing a sunny and protected children's play yard. The formal rear court includes a built-in-barbecue, a dining area, a fire pit, a spa and an infinity pool. In warm weather a series of oversized pivot doors open the living and dining spaces completely to the back garden.

From the parking area a path of flagstone steps leads to the main entrance into the living room, with tantalizing glimpses of the vista. The irregular shape of the pavers contrasts with the straight lines of the house, inserting an organic note.

In the interior, the stair core creates a boundary between formal and family functions on the ground and upper floors, and the zones can be closed off from each other by pocket doors. The cantilevered terrace of the master bedroom shades the outdoor dining area beneath; the diagonal of the terrace roof is aligned with the infinity edge of the pool.

Materials include poured concrete floors stained with brown pigment, custom walnut and white laminate cabinets and shelving, and white troweled stucco. In the living room the dropped ceiling of wood panels hides lighting fixtures and sound equipment.

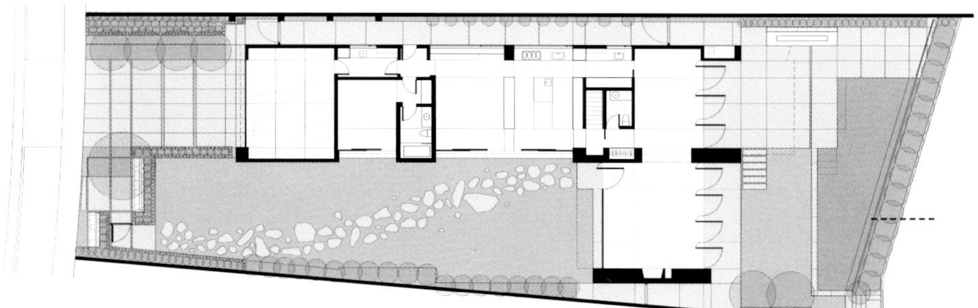

first floor plan

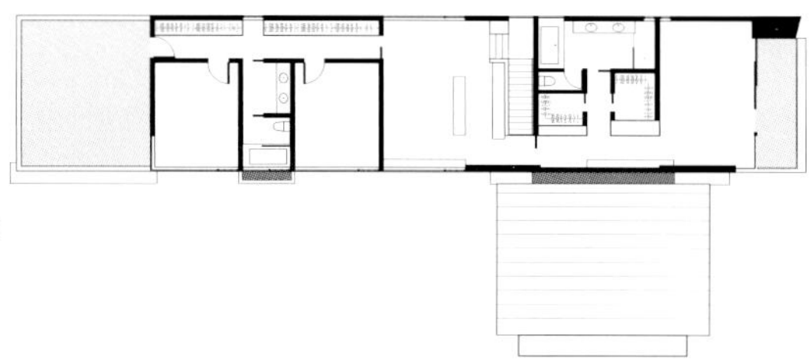

second floor plan

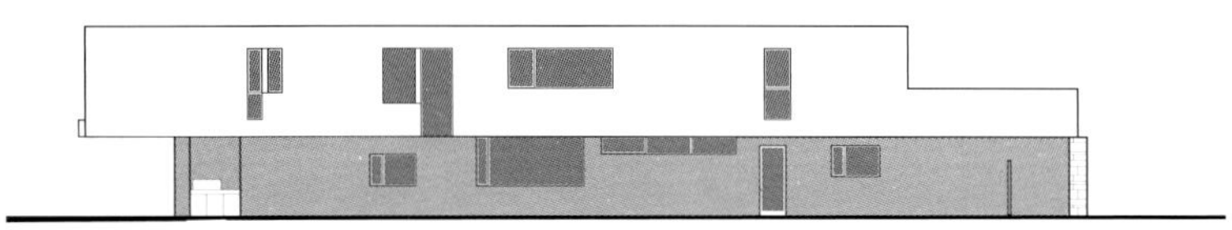

north elevation

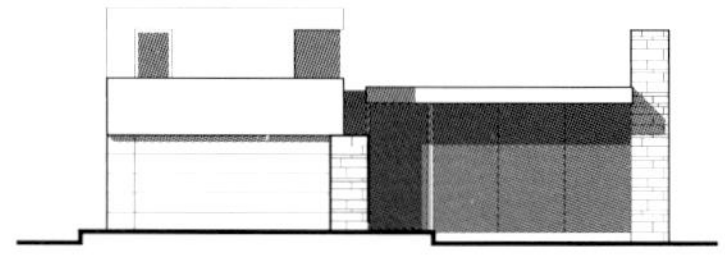

east elevation

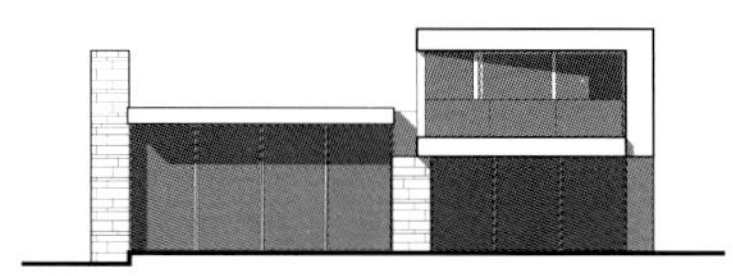

west elevation

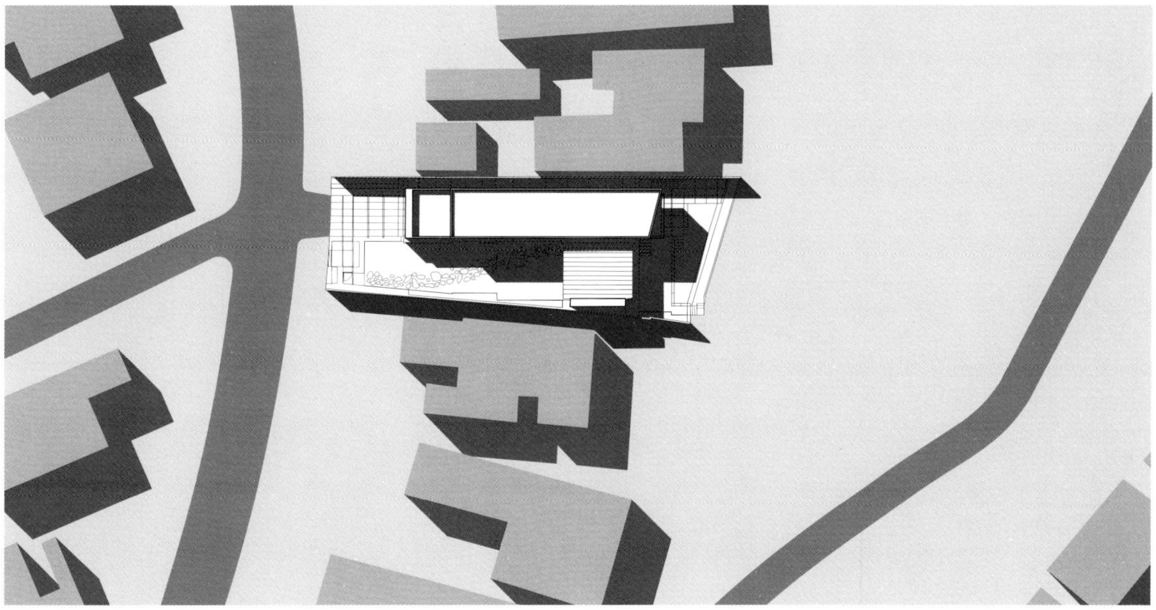
site plan

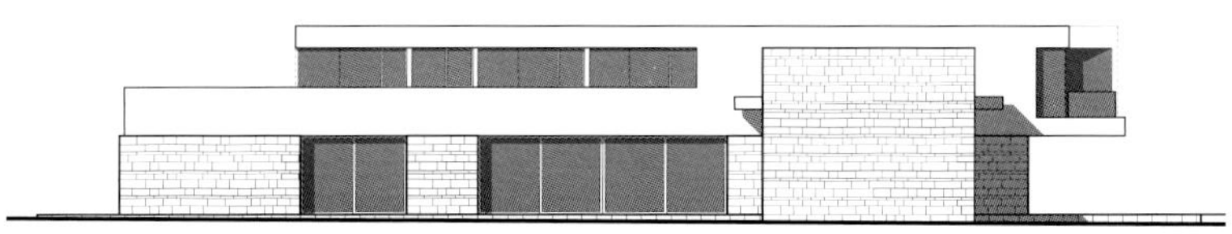
south elevation

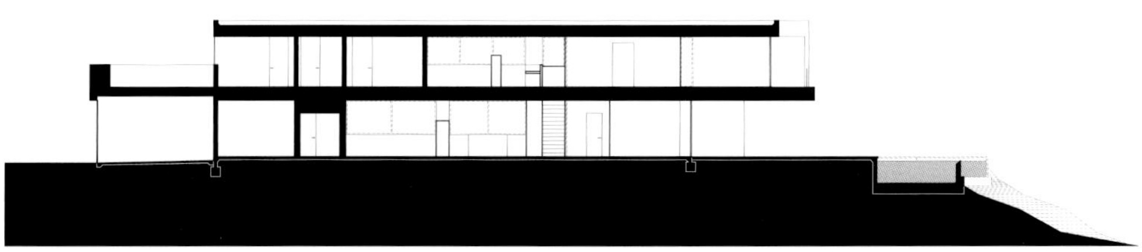
section

Carrillo Residence

Carrillo Residence

Carrillo Residence

1950

Wolfe Residence

Los Angeles, California

This unique house is exuberantly out of Africa. The clients, an African art dealer and big game hunter and his wife, asked for a sustainable dwelling in which to showcase their ever-changing collection of African art and furniture, as well as serve as a comfortable family home for them and two teen-aged sons. Sharing with Ehrlich a long history and love affair with Africa, the three collaborated on the exterior design, earthy interior details, and landscaping which all pay homage to that continent.

The pitched-roof structure looms above the bungalows and more conventional modern homes on its flat urban street in West Los Angeles. The shape and naturally weathering corrugated Cor-Ten steel reference African vernacular corrugated steel buildings, which have replaced traditional mud-and thatch-roofed huts. The classic gable roof becomes a gambrel at the front of the house, overhanging and defining the entrance.

Large glass pocket doors open the house to hardscape and plantings on one side and a pool court at the back. The doors, operable windows and exposed ceilings maximize cross-ventilation and reduce the need for air-conditioning.

Fourteen-foot high walls and stained poured-in-place concrete floors in the main living space provide a backdrop for African objects from many regions, including paintings, movie posters, standing sculptures and furniture. Tarantula imprints imbedded in the floor in a few places add a touch of whimsy. An open kitchen permits the hunter of the house to interact with guests as he prepares meals centering on whatever fresh game he has brought home, often wild boar, buffalo, or lobster.

A big game theme and safari spirit permeate the entire house. Zebra-print carpeting leads to the upper floor and mezzanine, past a skylit moosehead hanging on the stairwell wall—a trophy bagged by the owner. In the master bedroom, which features a balcony overlooking the backyard pool, a bison-head gazes down from the wall. The outdoors is xeriscaped with native plants and bark and sand ground cover. Poolside concrete terraces display African hardwood stools mixed with found and recycled artifacts, along with huge black and white boulders from Ghana.

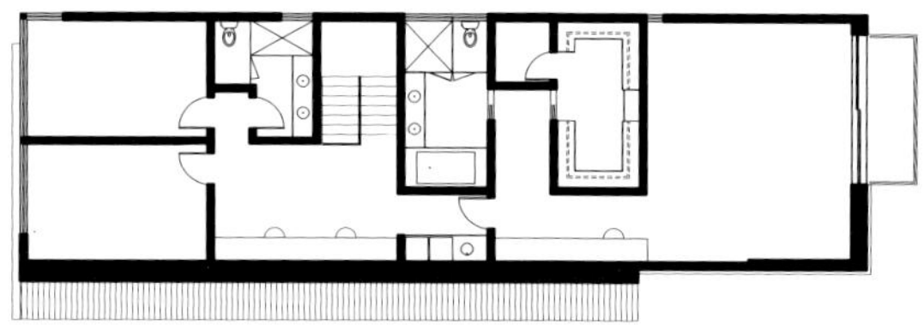

second floor plan

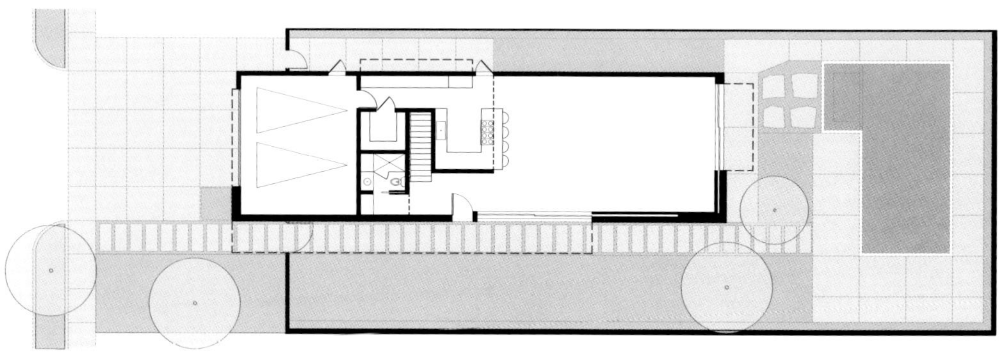

first floor plan

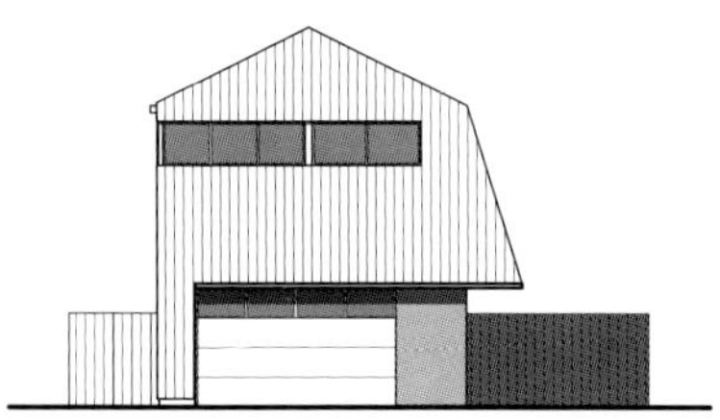

west elevation

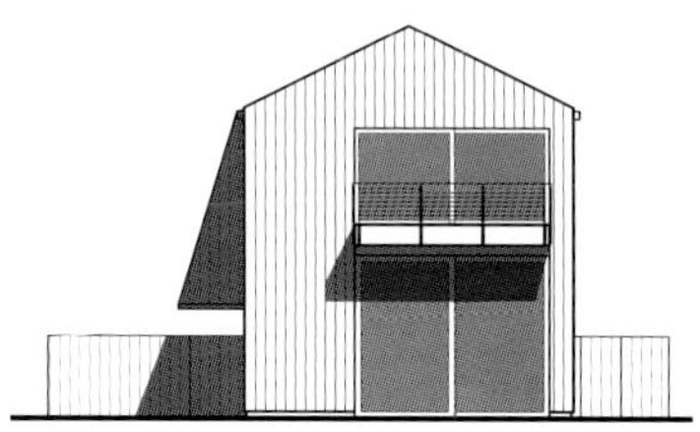

east elevation

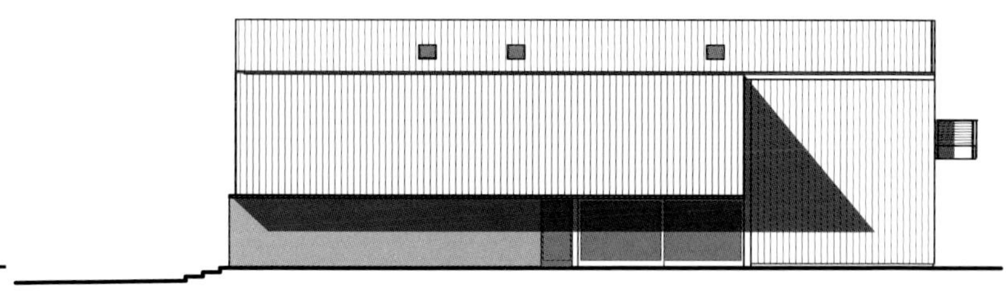

south elevation

site plan

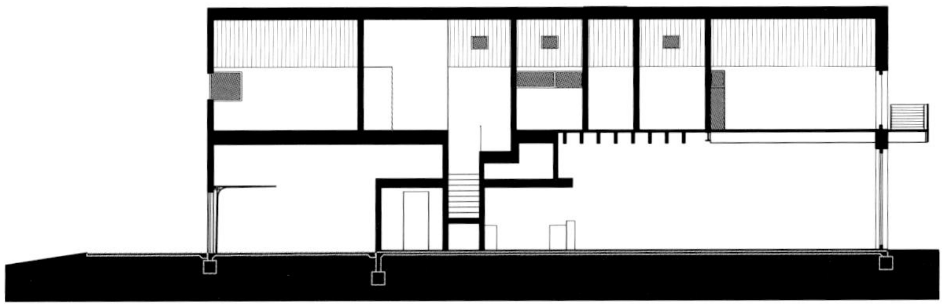

section

Wolfe Residence

Helal Residence

Helal Residence

United Arab Emirates

In this 35,000-square-foot house for a businessman and his family, Ehrlich reinterpreted traditional Islamic forms on a grand scale, cooling the scorching desert property with pools, palm trees, and a massive shade roof. The result is a palace of incomparable splendor set within an oasis, sensitively attuned to its cultural context and climate.

The compound consists of a series of two-story buildings, sheltered by a massive curved roof sheathed in shimmering aluminum. In profile, the canopy forms a crescent moon, the important symbol of new life that often tops Islamic minarets. Fourteen travertine-clad columns support and pierce through the roof, alluding to the traditional Arabic mud towers that captured wind currents. The whole structure suggests a giant Bedouin tent, with its football-sized roof cantilevering outward thirty feet on each side.

The L-shaped floor plan is organized according to Muslim custom, with a men's majlis or receiving area occupying its own wing, and a separate entrance framed in panels of translucent onyx. A women's majlis, the largest room in the house, is hidden behind the main entry hall and overlooks an enormous pool and date palm grove in the back garden. A traditional moucharabie (lattice screen), updated in cast aluminum, curves around the front facade. The screen filters the intense sunlight and casts dappled shadows of Islamic star patterns onto the stone floors and reflecting pool, which weaves in and out of the monumental entrance hall.

Surrounding the buildings is a lush sequence of pools, gardens, fountains, courtyards, and terraces that creates a microclimate and contributes to cooling by evaporation. The counterpoint between ancient and modern is reinforced throughout the house by the juxtaposition of massive stone walls, large expanses of glass, and taut elements of steel. In the family wing, two master bedrooms open completely on two sides at the corner with sliding glass doors, connecting the interior to the landscape. Above the bedrooms, open-air porches encourage sleeping and star-gazing under the protection of the grand crescent roof.

Helal Residence

Helal Residence

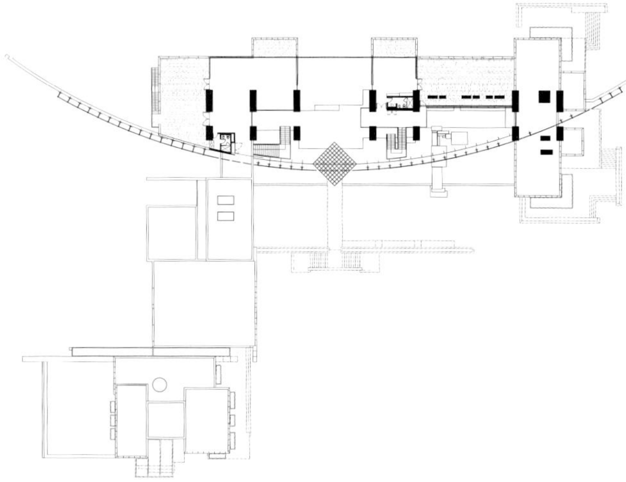

second floor plan

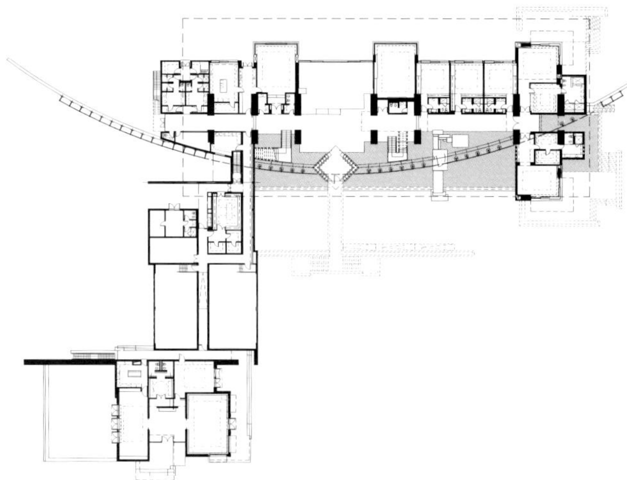

first floor plan

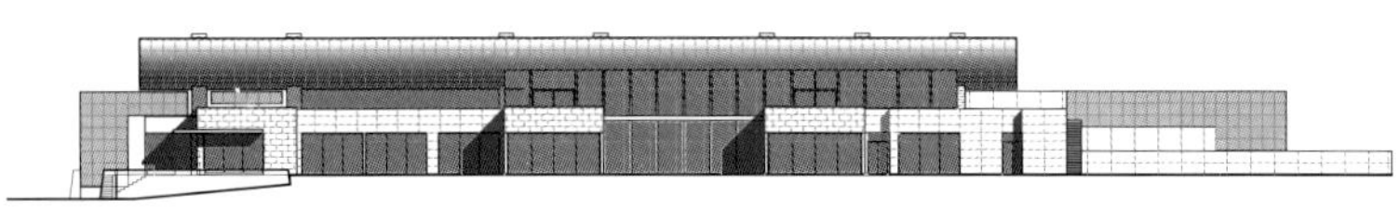

north elevation

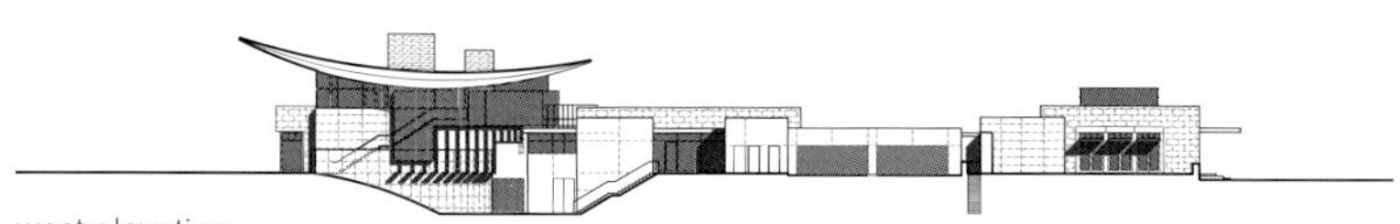

west elevation

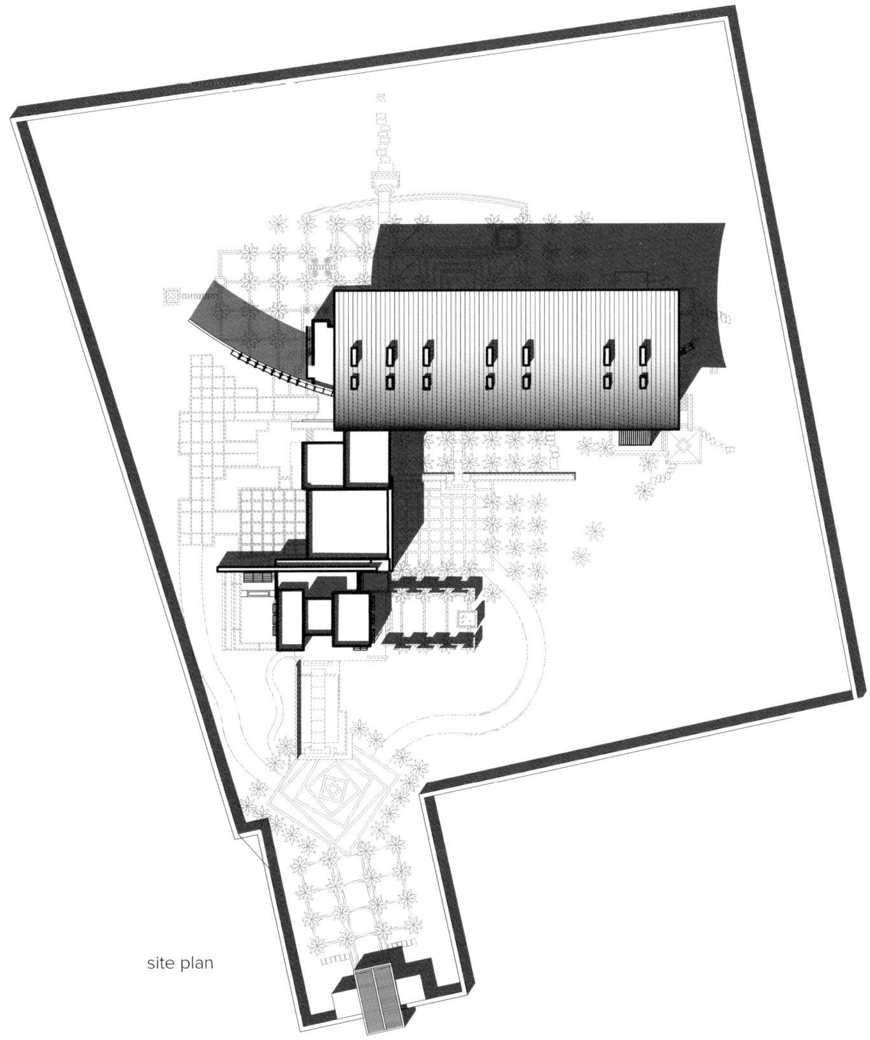

site plan

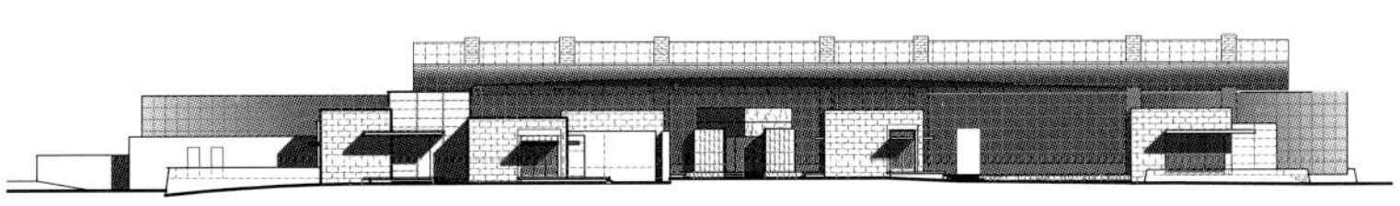

south elevation

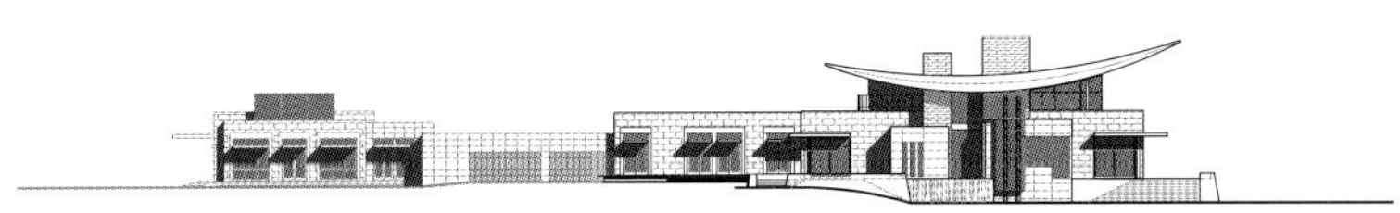

east elevation

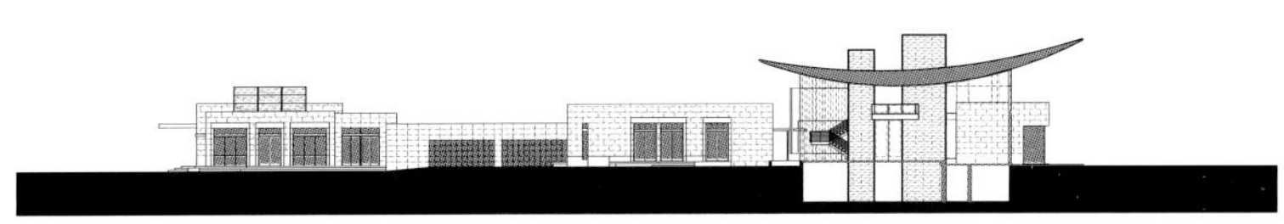

section

Helal Residence

Kreuzer-Schroeder Residence

Houston, Texas

A professional couple purchased a two-acre site in an exclusive neighborhood where houses are typically traditional, with grand entrances oriented toward the street. The clients opted for something different, beginning with their decision to install a driveway locating their house deep within the wooded, flat property, making it invisible from the road.

They asked Ehrlich and Yanai to design a modern house providing California-style indoor-outdoor living—to the degree possible in Houston's harsh climate, where summers are hot and humid and winters are wet. The mostly one-story plan takes advantage of the large site and creates strong connections to the outdoors with large expanses of glass interspersed with limestone masses. Dining and entertaining areas feature floor-to-ceiling glass pivot doors. The master bedroom, master bath and study all open out to secluded gardens. A two-story children's wing with playroom, music room and study area overlooks a double-height family great room.

Summer heat and heavy rainfall are mitigated with deep roof overhangs and slatted sunscreens shielding glazed surfaces. Materials include Texas limestone and Rheinzink, with poured concrete floors and custom back-painted glass cabinets indoors. At the entrance court, a large Rheinzink wall which morphs into the garage doors separates guest parking from the house, insuring tranquility in the house and gardens.

There is a separate guest/pool house with its own private garden.

first floor plan

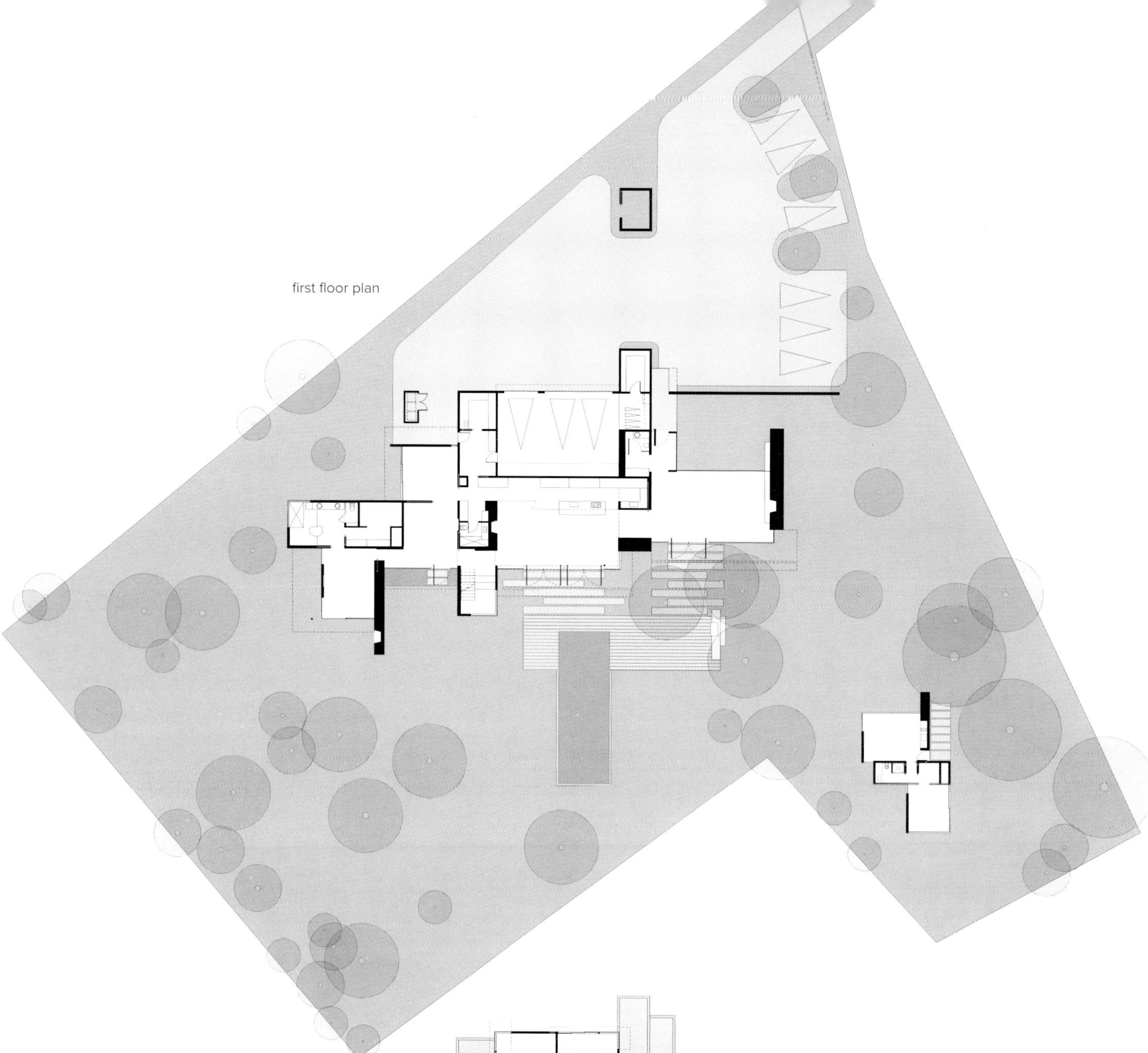

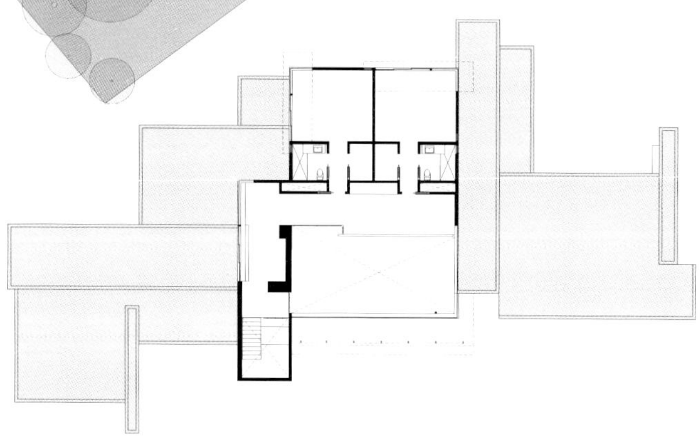

second floor plan

40'/12m

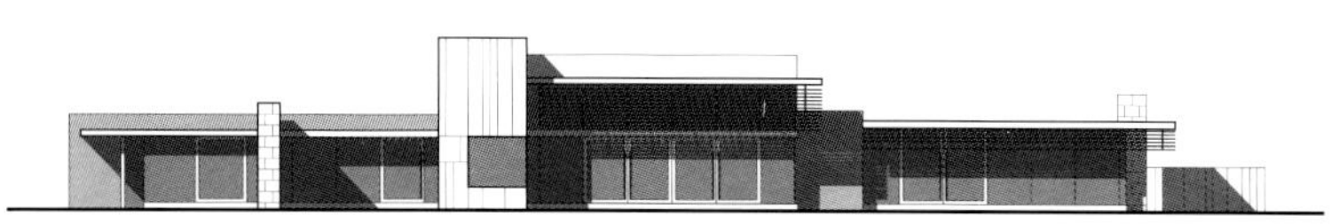

south elevation

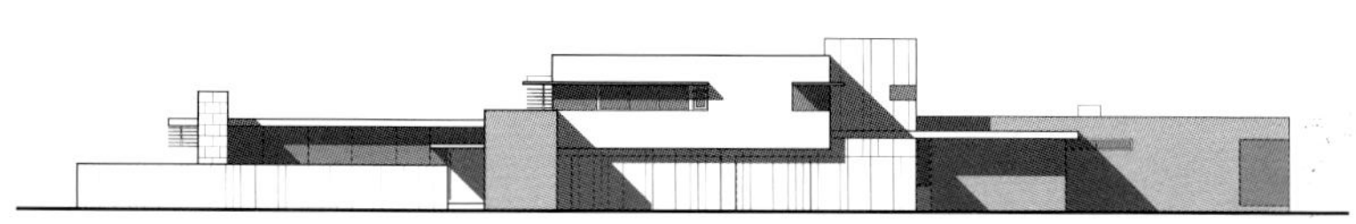

north elevation

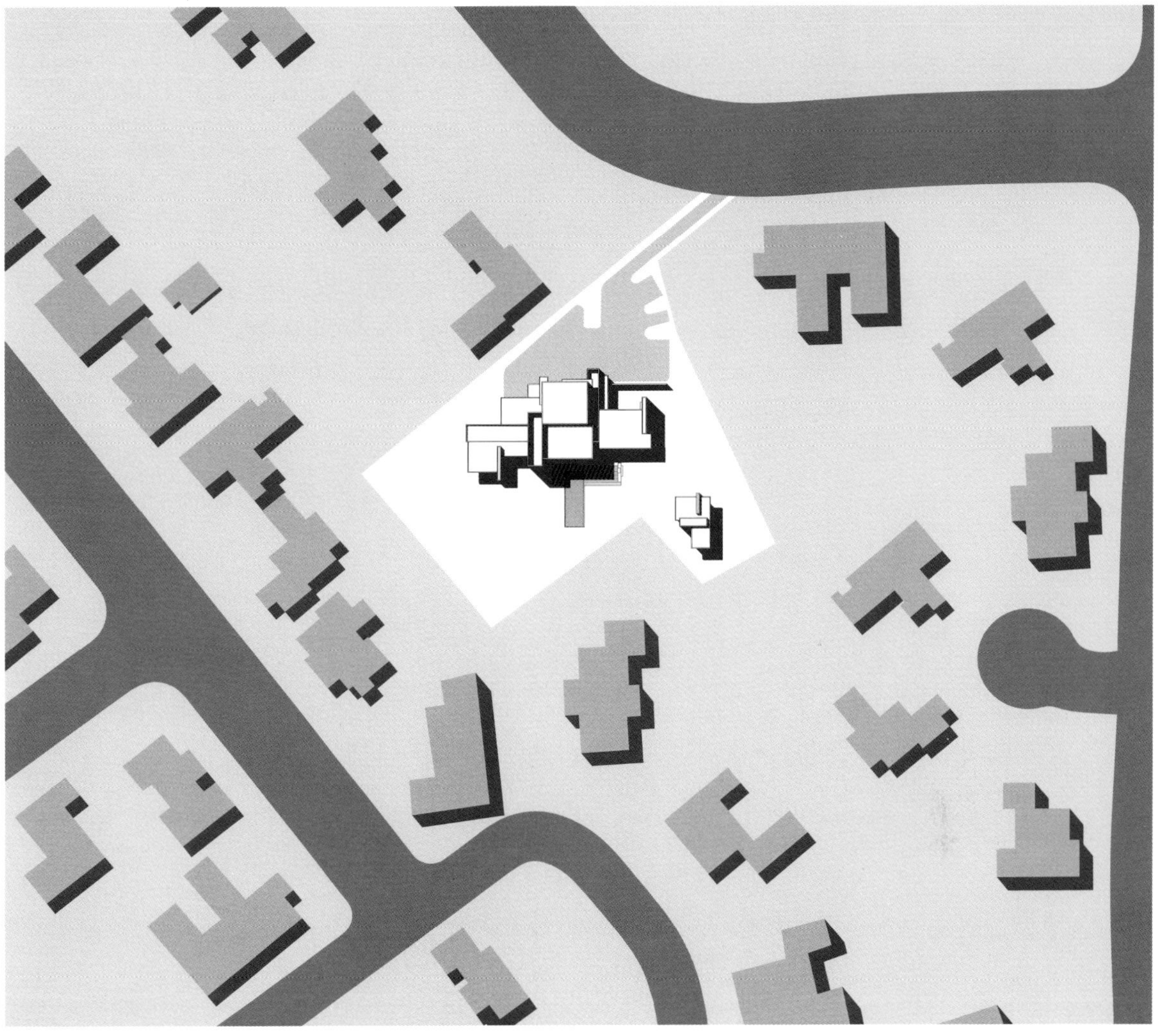

site plan

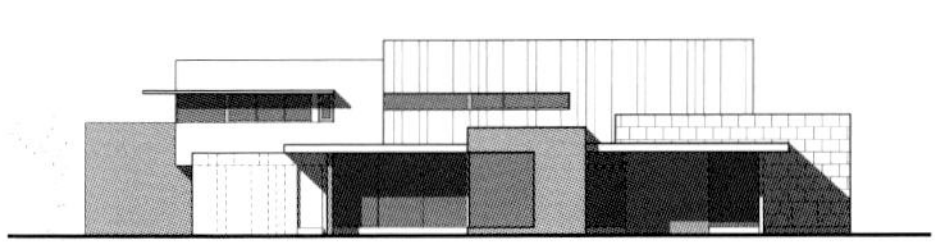

west elevation

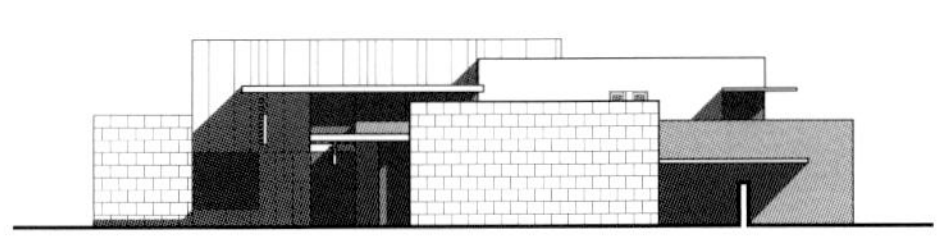

east elevation

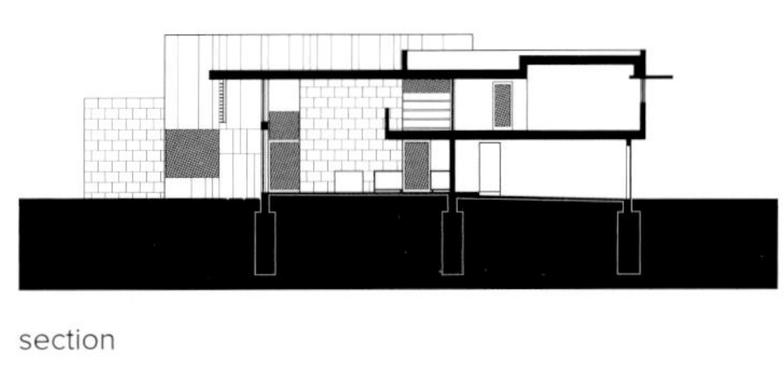

section

Kreuzer-Schroeder Residence

McElroy Residence

Laguna Beach, California

Nestled at the end of a cul-de-sac in a private southern California beach community, this house commands spectacular vistas of the Pacific Ocean. In creating a home for a couple with two sons who enjoy outdoor living and entertaining, the architects' brief was to provide gracious and open spaces and simultaneously orchestrate the views, despite an eleven-foot height limit imposed by the homeowners association.

Ehrlich and Yanai's design solution makes a virtue of horizontality: the house is an expansive series of spaces underneath a giant floating horizontal roof plane which is supported on stone masses, wood walls, and slender steel columns. Oversized sliding glass doors pocket completely away to dissolve the physical boundaries between interior and exterior, creating an uninterrupted flow from the rear courtyard through the main living space to the pool area, all against the backdrop of the Pacific Ocean.

The compound is entered along a fifty-foot long sustainable-growth hardwood (ipe) wall. Guest and children's bedrooms open onto a protected courtyard in the rear, while the master suite commands a layered view over the swimming pool and seascape beyond. The master bath opens onto its own private meditation garden.

The massive walls of stacked limestone, a counterpoint to the structure's strong horizontality, form fireplaces in the interior. A variety of outdoor living and entertaining spaces are composed by stone floors that extend outside, together with decks, concrete and landscaping. The main garden space includes a pool, with an adjacent sitting area with fireplace sheltered by a roof canopy.

The garage, workout room, storage and service areas are all located in the basement—freeing up the entire ground floor for maximum enjoyment of the Southern California climate and lifestyle.

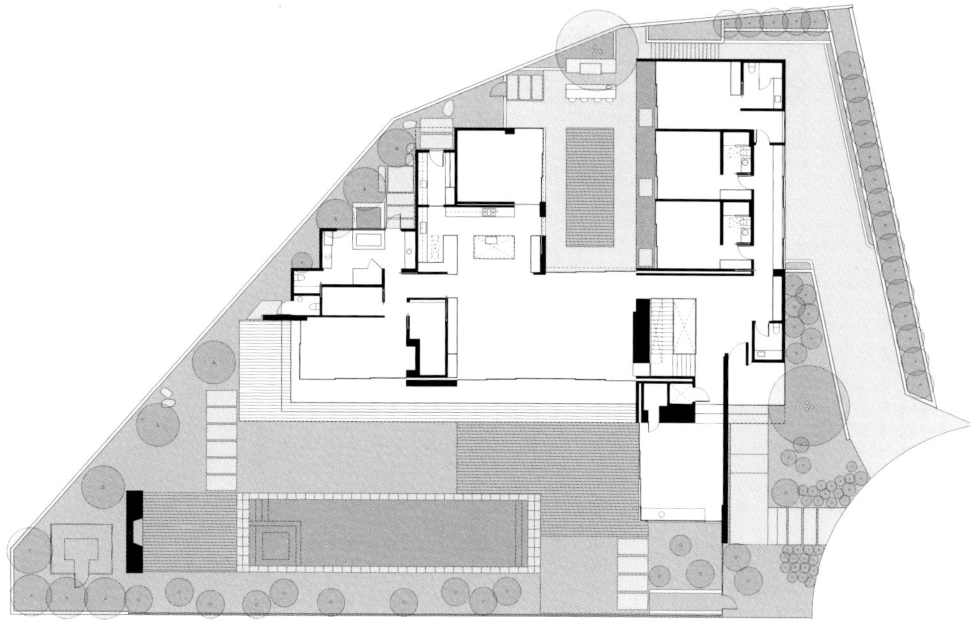

first floor plan

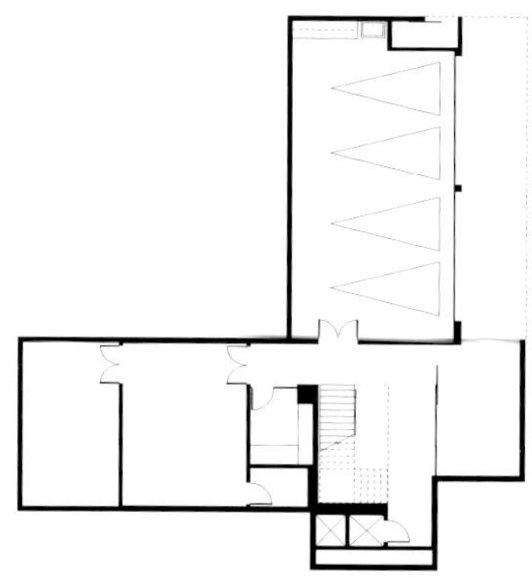

basement plan

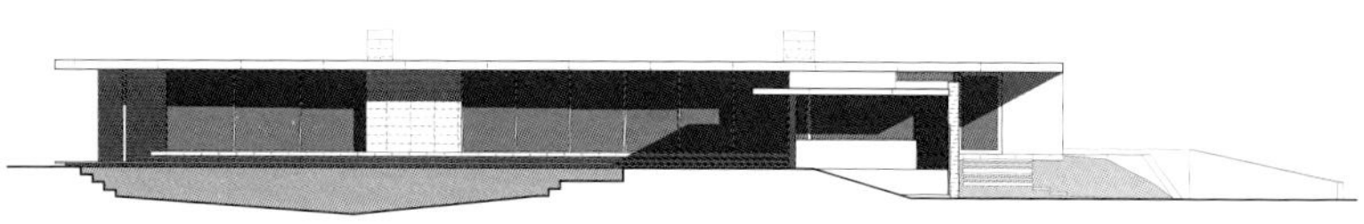

south elevation

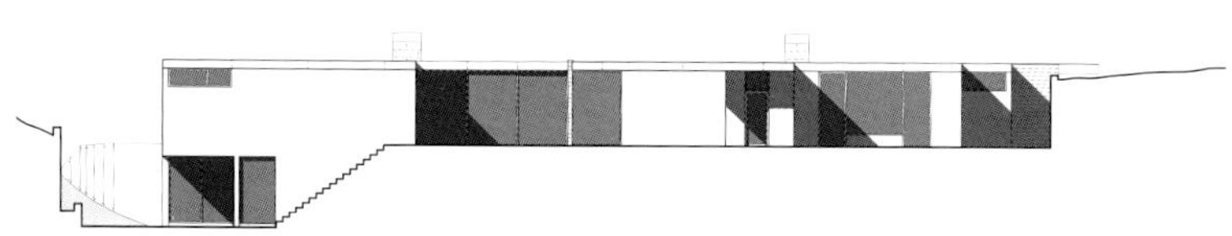

north elevation

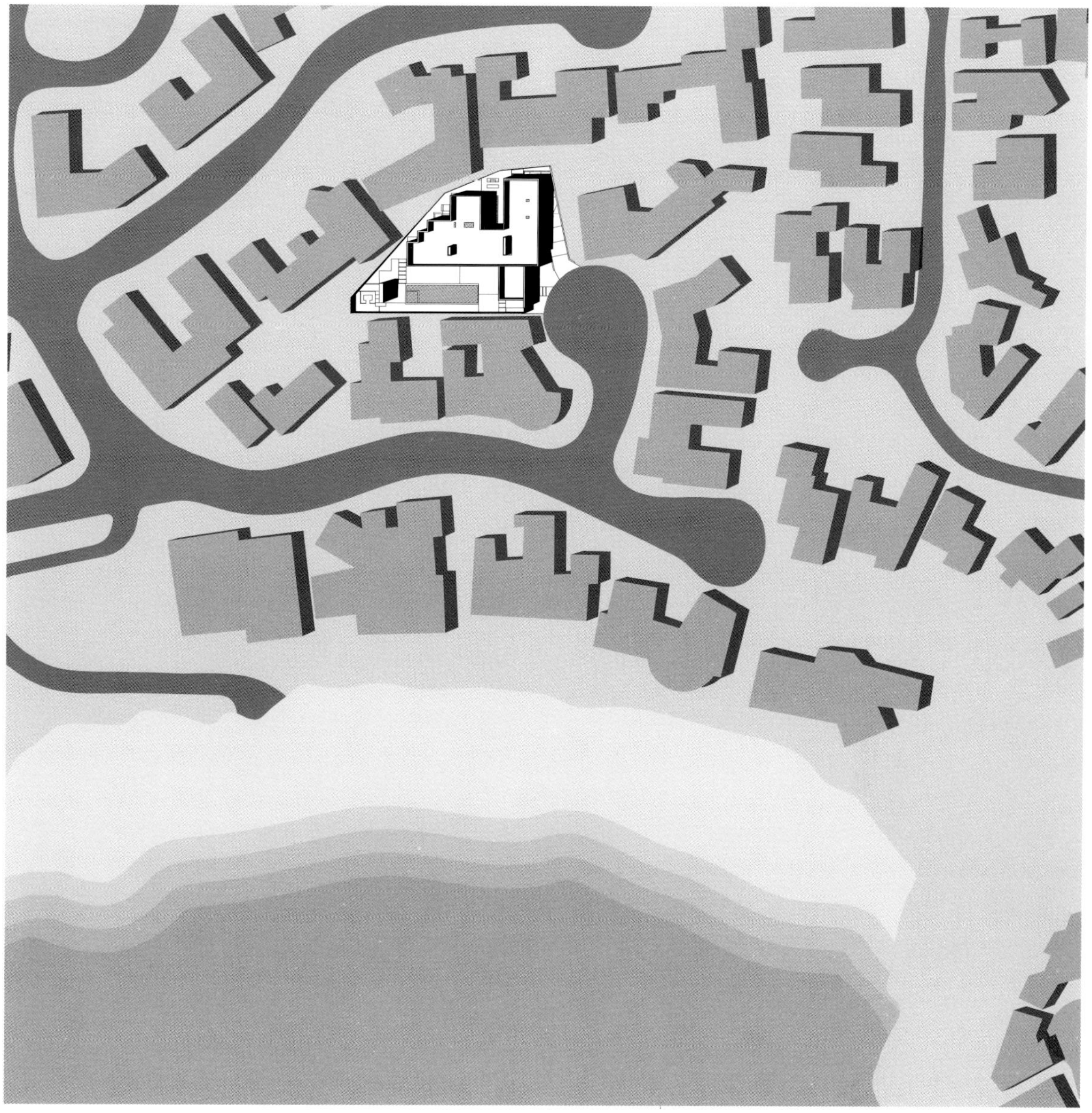

site plan

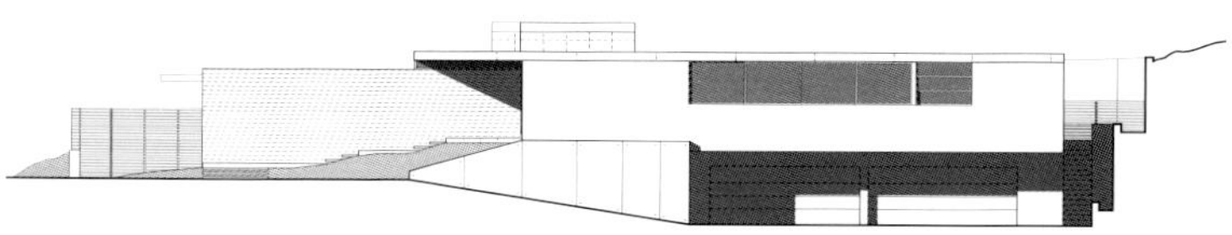

east elevation

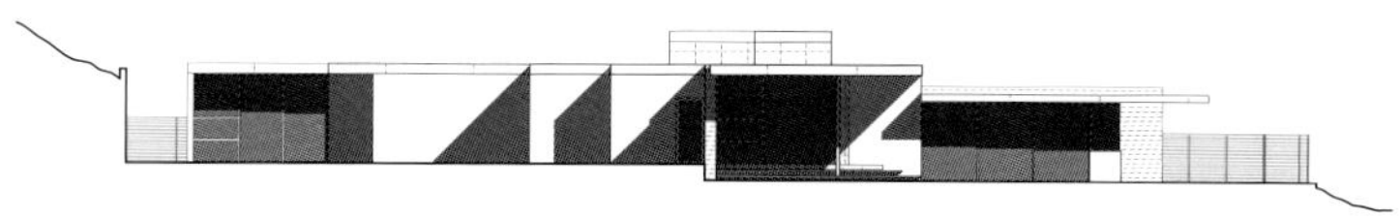

west elevation

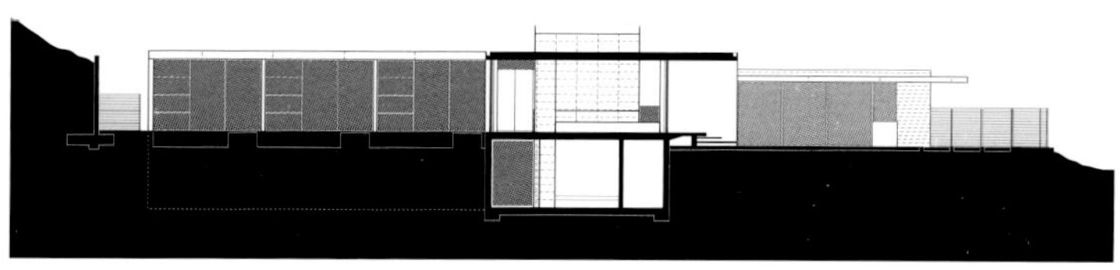

section

McElroy Residence

MacMillan Residence

Palm Desert, California

This house in the San Jacinto Mountains echoes the subtle beauty of its desert location and accentuates breathtaking views of the surrounding Coachella Valley. Built for a retired couple with grown children and a museum-quality art collection, the house is perched on a stone plinth cut from the rocky terrain. Its low profile and strong horizontal rooflines establish its pedigree as a descendant of mid-century desert modern houses in nearby Palm Springs.

The house is comprised of three main wings—the master suite, main living and guest bedroom wings—each of which is defined by a giant roof plane that folds down to form a side wall, establishing privacy among them. The fascias and walls of these folding planes are bronze, and a continuous bronze roof band that runs around the perimeter of the house is a unifying element.

In the grand central space, defined by the largest of the folded planes, are the main living, dining and kitchen areas. Floating in this volume is a tilted gold leaf cone within which is a private sitting area. The cone pierces through a circular skylight, allowing natural light to pour inside the cone.

In all three wings, glass corners offer unobstructed panoramic valley views. Oversized glass doors slide open and terrazzo floors spill outdoors, creating a generous terrace that runs the length of the building and is sheltered by deep roof overhangs. A glass-edged infinity pool anchors the terrace and defines the horizon line.

The house harmonizes with its habitat through an abundant use of local stone.

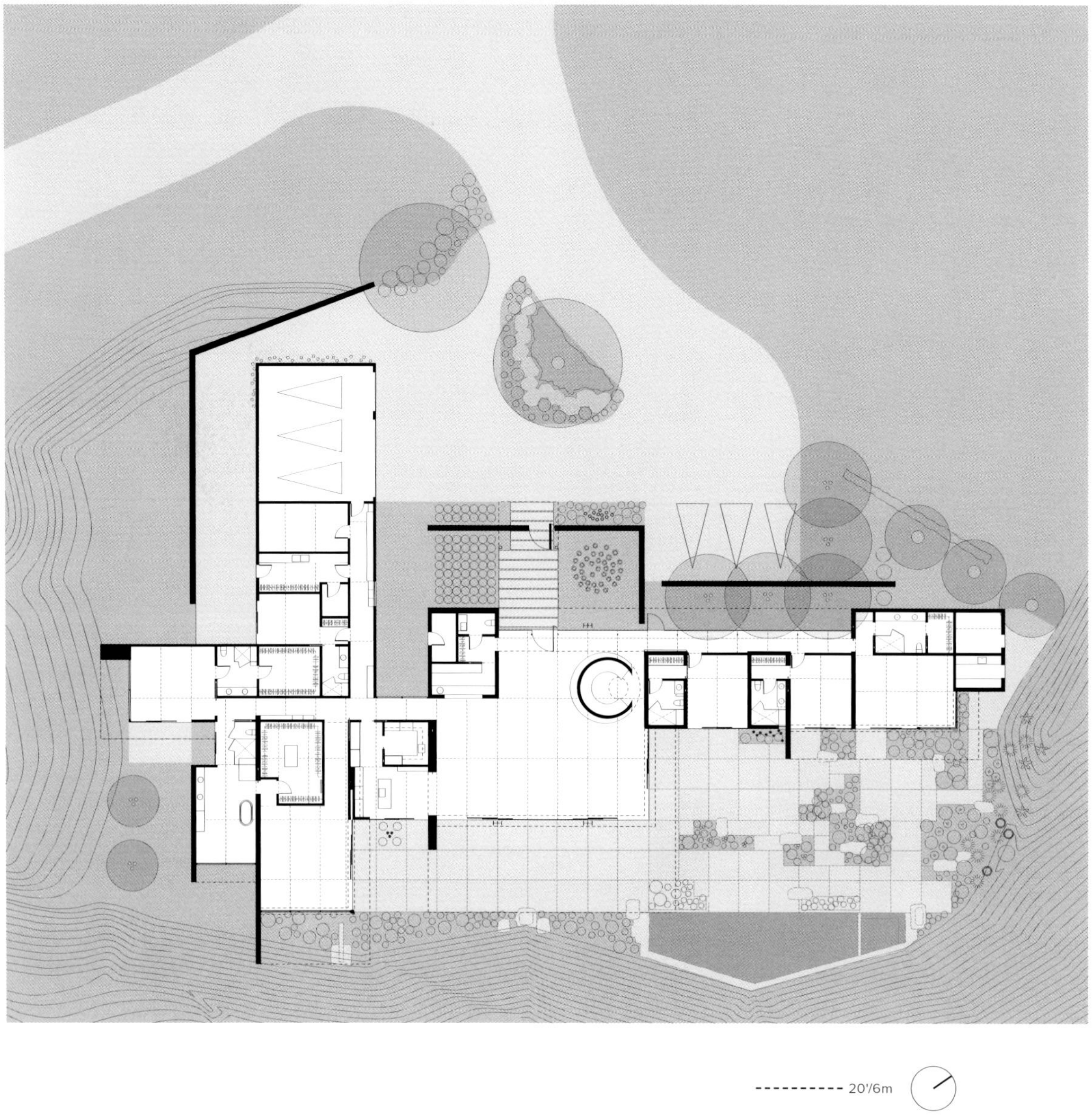

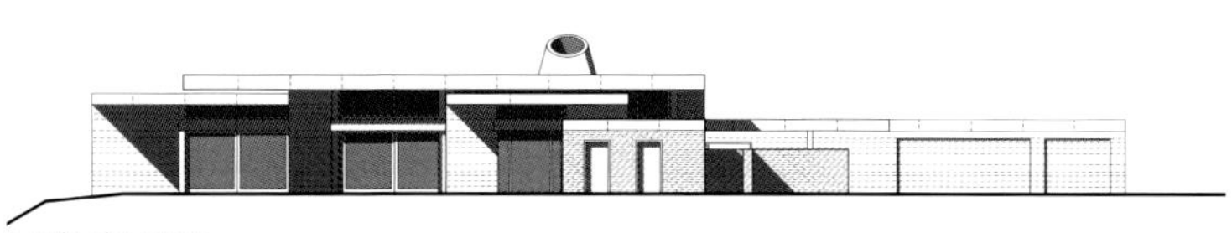

north elevation

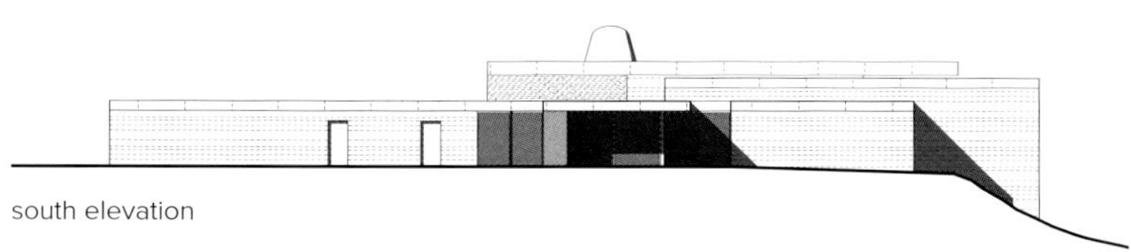

south elevation

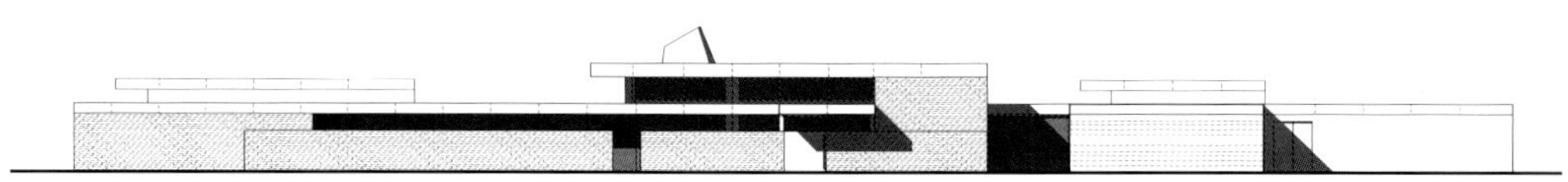

west elevation

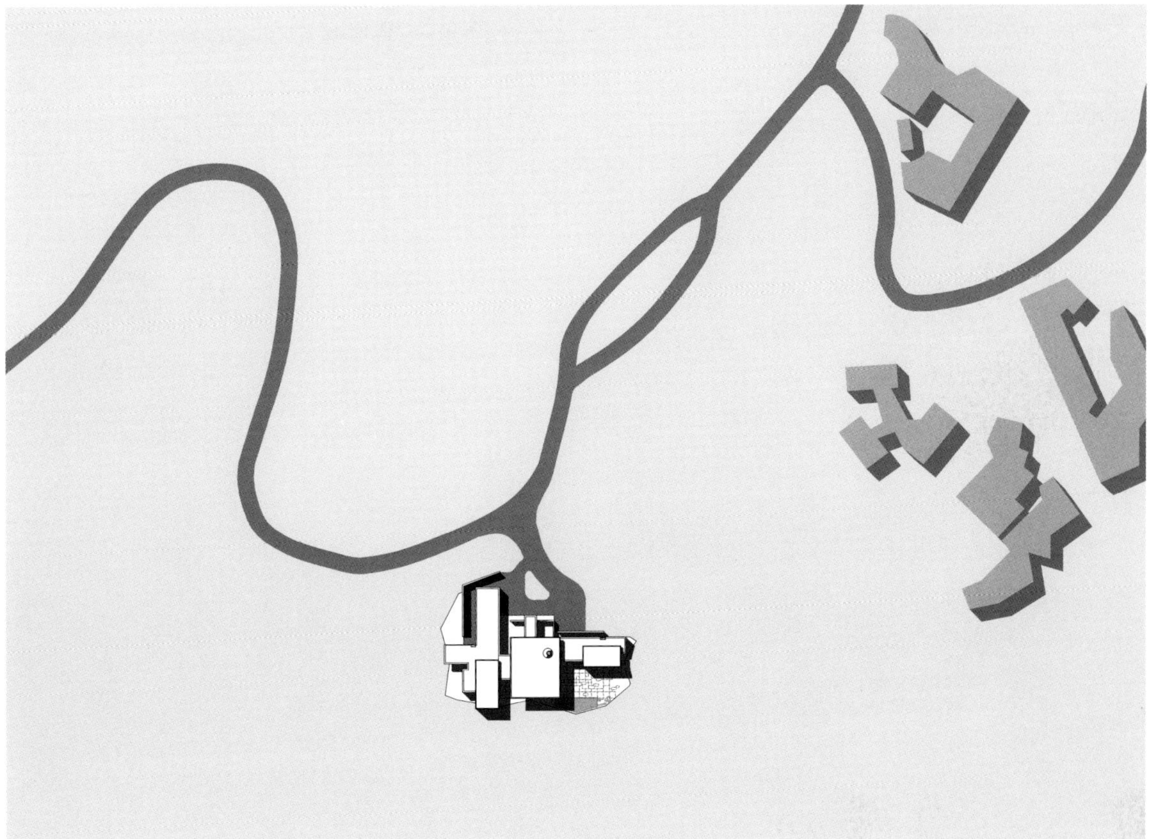

site plan

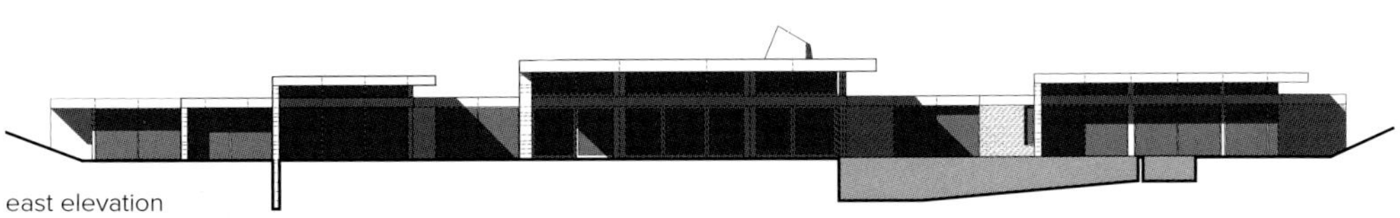

east elevation

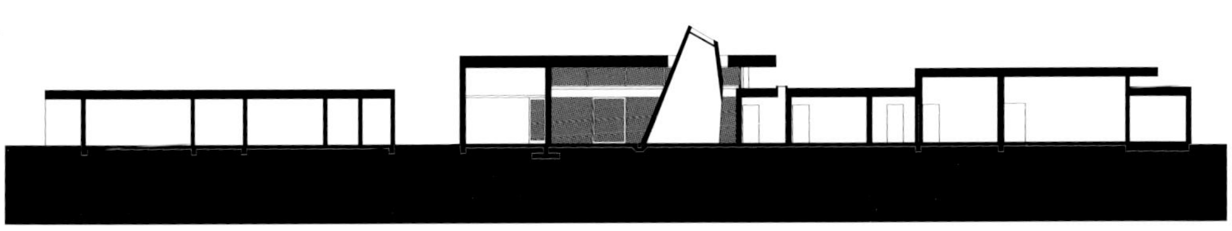

section

Credits and acknowledgments

Project credits

Kalfus Studio / 1981
Client: Renee and Jordan Kalfus
Design principal: Steven Ehrlich
Construction manager: Steven Ehrlich

Addition to Neutra Beach House / 1998
Client: John Law and Hope Warschaw
Design principal: Steven Ehrlich
Project architect: James Schmidt
Project team: Nick Seierup, Brent Eckerman, Tim Champ, Supachai Kiatkwankul, Todd Flournoy, Pierre Paley, Troy Williams, Jonathon Riddle, Juergen Zimmerman, Tina Hollenbacher
Landscape architect: Beer + Associates
Lighting: Edward Effron
General contractor: Lautenschlager Inc.

Schindler House on Ellis Avenue / 2010
Client: Onna Ehrlich and Joel Bell
Original architect: Rudolf M. Schindler
Design principal: Steven Ehrlich
Project manager: Joel Bell
Landscape architect: Hammerschmidt & Lidow, Landscape Design
Lighting: Bill Gonzales/David Silverman& Associates, Inc.
Furniture: Provided by Friends of the Schindler House
General contractor: Shramek Building Co.
Master craftsman: Jesus Maldonado

700 Palms Residence / 2005
Client: Steven Ehrlich and Nancy Griffin
Design principal: Steven Ehrlich
Project manager: Mathew Chaney
Project team: Thomas E. Zahlten, Justin Brechtel, Magdalena Glen-Schieneman, Michael Pardek, Steffen Doelger, Yoshiaki Irie and Nicole Pflug
Landscape architect: Jay Griffith + Stefan Hammerschmidt
Site-specific artist: Woods Davey
General contractor: Shramek Building Co.

Webster Residence / 2002
Client: James Webster
Design principal: Steven Ehrlich
Principal-in-charge: James Schmidt
Project team: George Elian, Justin Brechtel, Simone Barth, David Mangini, Michael Pardek
Landscape architect: Jay Griffith
General contractor: Shramek Building Co.

Boxenbaum Residence / 2005
Client: Chuck & Kharlene Boxenbaum
Design principal: Steven Ehrlich
Principal-in-charge: Takashi Yanai
Project team: James Schmidt, George Elian, Thomas Hanley, Alec Whitten, Magdalena Glen-Schieneman
Landscape architect: Nancy Goslee Power & Associates
Lighting: Integrated Lighting Design
General contractor: Horizon General Contractors

Schulman Residence / 1992
Client: Tom and Miriam Schulman
Design principal: Steven Ehrlich
Project team: Melvyn Bernstein, James Schmidt, Carlos Kitzinger
Landscape architect: Robert Cornell & Associates
Interior design: Luis Ortega Design Studio
General contractor: Winters-Schram Associates

Canyon Residence / 1998
Design principal: Steven Ehrlich
Project architect: James Schmidt
Project team: Brent Eckerman, Eric Hammerlund, Supachai Kiatkwankul, Thomas E. Zahlten, Scott Hunter, Pierre Paley, Alec Whitten Frederic LeClercq, Un-Ju Choi, Stefanie Hinsen, Troy Williams, Pierre Paley
Landscape architect: Griffith and Zarraga
Interior design: Philippa Seth-Smith
Lighting: Edward Effron & Associates
General contractor: C.E.R. Development, Inc.

Waldfogel Residence / 2006
Client: Asher Waldfogel and Helyn MacLean
Design principal: Steven Ehrlich
Principal-in-charge: Takashi Yanai
Project team: James Schmidt, Alec Whitten, George Elian, Edward Rolen, Haekwan Park
Landscape architect: Conger Moss Guillard
Interior design: Mike Witt
Construction managers: Ted Horten, Larry McClure
General contractor: Ryan Associates

Zeidler Residence / 2008
Client: Leland and Marian Zeidler
Design principal: Steven Ehrlich
Principal-in-charge: Takashi Yanai
Project team: James Schmidt, Mary Chou, Lisa Donnerhack
Landscape architect: SSA Landscape Architects, Inc.
General contractor: George A. Fitch Construction

Leonard Residence / 2005
Client: Josh and Linda Leonard
Design principal: Steven Ehrlich
Principal-in-charge: James Schmidt
Project team: George Elian, Alec Whitten, Justin Brechtel, Ed Rolen
General contractor: Horizon General Contractors

Carrillo Residence / 2010
Client: Juan Carrillo and Dominique Mielle
Design principal: Steven Ehrlich
Principal-in-charge: Takashi Yanai
Project team: Jacqueline Park, Ryan Lobello
Landscape architect: Barry Beer Design
Lighting: e^2 Lighting Design
General contractor: Horizon General Contractors, Inc.

Wolfe Residence / 2009
Client: Ernie and Diane Wolfe
Design principal: Steven Ehrlich
Principal-in-charge: Takashi Yanai
Project team: Becky Nix, Ryan Lobello, Karli Molter
General contractor: Decoma Industries

Helal Residence / 2006
Design principal: Steven Ehrlich
Project team: James Schmidt, Thomas Hanley
Executive architect: Godwin Austen Johnson; Brian Johnson, principal; Jason Burnside, project architect
Landscape architect: Al Khatib Cracknel
Lighting: Maurice Brill Lighting Design Ltd.
Interior design: Hirsch Bedner Associates
General contractor: ASCON

McElroy Residence
Client: Thom and Sarah McElroy
Design principal: Steven Ehrlich
Principal-in-charge: Takashi Yanai
Project team: Brendan Canning, Jacqueline Park, Ryan Lobello, Carl Paatz, Lindsey Davis, Guelsah Kuecuek
Landscape architect: LA Studio
Lighting: e^2 Lighting Design
General contractor: Buwalda Construction

Kreuzer-Schroeder Residence
Client: Stefan Kreuzer and Barbara Schroeder
Design principal: Steven Ehrlich
Principal-in-charge: Takashi Yanai
Project team: Brendan Canning, Jacqueline Park, Noah Marble, Guelsah Kuecuek, Lindsey Davis,
General contractor: Builders West, Inc.

MacMillan Residence
Client: Donna and Cargill MacMillan
Design principal: Steven Ehrlich
Principal-in-charge: Takashi Yanai
Project team: Brendan Canning, Jacqueline Park, Guelsah Kuecuek, Jesie Kelly
General contractor: DeWitte Construction

Acknowledgments

Designing and building houses was my first love as an architect, and remains as rewarding today as when I opened my practice thirty years ago. That is because we at Ehrlich Architects have been blessed with clients who are great people, and whose imagination and intelligence has always challenged us. The architect-residential client relationship is an intimate one that is built on mutual respect and a shared willingness to embark on an exciting journey together. This book is dedicated to you, our co-adventurers.

The team

All of the houses in these pages are the result of collaborative effort. I am profoundly fortunate to work with a team whose professionalism and talents are unsurpassed. Thanks to every member of the Ehrlich Architects family as well as former staff who helped bring the projects to life.

First and foremost I must salute the head of our Residential Studio Takashi Yanai, AIA, whose superb design skills and leadership are manifest in these projects. Takashi has been ably supported by the creative efforts of designers Brendan Canning, Noah Marble, and Guelsha Kuecuek. Our graphic designer Ann-Christine Pineiro performed the indispensable task of coordinating and reviewing the project, compiling images from our archives.

I wish to acknowledge my steadfast partners, each of whom deserves so much credit for the success of our firm: Principals Takashi Yanai, AIA; Thomas E. Zahlten, AIA, and Charles "Duke" Oakley, FAIA. I also want to thank Director of Development Rachel Morel who consistently and effectively represents our work to the international publication community.

The clients

Heartfelt thanks to all of you for putting your faith in us.

The collaborators

We are indebted to the landscape architects, engineers, contractors and artisans who have richly contributed in so many ways.

The editor

I owe this book's existence to Elizabeth White, who believed in this project and promoted it at The Monacelli Press. I am deeply grateful for her unflagging enthusiasm and attention to every detail.

The book designer

Thanks to David Blankenship for showcasing the houses so beautifully in his inspired layouts.

The photographers

To the wizards who capture magical images of light on form, thank you all.

The writers

I am honored by the insights and historical perspective Sam Lubell brought to writing the introduction. Thanks (always) to Nancy Griffin for her words and wisdom.

Illustration credits

Russell Abraham: 147, 157
BioLINIA: 222-223, 226-227, 230-231
Tom Bonner: 96-97, 100-101, 104-105
Benny Chan: 68, 70-73, 76-79
Grey Crawford: 48-53, 60-61, 162, 164-167, 171
Ehrlich Architects: 20-21, 30-31, 43, 58-59, 74-75, 86-87, 102-103, 116-117, 130-131, 152-153, 168-169, 180-181, 198-199, 212-213, 224-225, 228-229, 232-233
Steven Ehrlich: 11 (top left, bottom), 23 (top and middle right, bottom), 47, 67 (top left and middle, bottom) 81, 95, 109, 123, 141 (top, middle left, bottom), 161, 173, 191, 203, 221
© J. Paul Getty Trust. Used with permission. Julius Shulman Photography Archive, Research Library at the Getty Research Institute (2004.R.10): 12, 14-19
Art Gray: 84-85, 88-89, 92-93
John Edward Linden: 28
Thomas Loof: 110-112, 114-115, 118-121
Luckhaus Studio: 23 (top left)
Matthew Millman: 2-3, 142, 144-146, 148-151, 154-156, 158-159
Matthew Millman / *Architectural Digest*; Copyright © Condé Nast: 126-129, 132, 138-139
Ministry du l'urbanisme et l'habitat Morocco: 67 (top right), 141 (middle right)
Grant Mudford: 35 (top right, middle and bottom), 36-42, 44-45, 192-197, 200-201
Mary E. Nichols / *Architectural Digest*; Copyright © Condé Nast: 98-99, 106
Juergen Nogai: 82-83, 90-91
Erhard Pfeiffer: 54-55, 64-65, 204-206, 208-211, 214-215, 218-219
Erhard Pfeiffer / *Architectural Digest*; Copyright © Condé Nast: 207, 216-217
Sharon Risedorph: 124-125, 133-137
Barry Schwartz: 174-179, 182-188
Julius Shulman & David Glomb: 24
Julius Shulman & Juergen Nogai: 56-57, 62-63
Tim Street-Porter: 11 (top right), 26-27, 29, 32-33, 35 (top left), 113, 189
Alan Weintraub: 107
Bradley Wheeler: 170